GOD, SCIENCE, AND SELF

MCGILL-QUEEN'S STUDIES IN MODERN ISLAMIC THOUGHT

Series Editors: Humeira Iqtidar and Muhammad Qasim Zaman

This series provides a platform for significant developments in the study of modern Islamic thought, now recognized for its richness, diversity, and possibility. It promotes scholarship that moves beyond binaries – traditional/modern, authentic/inauthentic, liberal/non-liberal – to engage with specific ideas, the creativity of modern Islamic thinkers, and their contributions to global ethical and political questions. Rather than assuming a singular Islamic response to contemporary issues, scholarship in this series explores the multiple perspectives of Islamic thinkers. McGill-Queen's Studies in Modern Islamic Thought focuses on the modern period, broadly defined as the eighteenth century to the present, to permit a sustained analysis of longue *durée* transformations in Islamic thought. It includes a geographically wide range of scholarship and supports new avenues of inquiry from intellectual and cultural history, political thought, political theory, and Islamic studies, which also transcend their disciplinary frameworks to lend greater depth and nuance to our understanding of ideas across different periods and contexts.

1 God, Science, and Self
Muhammad Iqbal's Reconstruction of Religious Thought
Nauman Faizi

God, Science, and Self

Muhammad Iqbal's Reconstruction of Religious Thought

NAUMAN FAIZI

McGill-Queen's University Press
Montreal & Kingston • London • Chicago

ISBN 978-0-2280-0658-9 (cloth)
ISBN 978-0-2280-0659-6 (paper)
ISBN 978-0-2280-0730-2 (ePDF)

Legal deposit third quarter 2021
Bibliothèque nationale du Québec

Printed in Canada on acid-free paper that is 100% ancient forest free
(100% post-consumer recycled), processed chlorine free

Library and Archives Canada Cataloguing in Publication

Title: God, science, and self : Muhammad Iqbal's Reconstruction of religious thought / Nauman Faizi.
Other titles: Muhammad Iqbal's Reconstruction of religious thought
Names: Faizi, Nauman, author.
Description: Series statement: Mcgill-Queen's studies in modern Islamic thought ; 1 | Includes bibliographical references and index.
Identifiers: Canadiana (print) 20210170840 | Canadiana (ebook) 20210171103 | ISBN 9780228006589 (cloth) | ISBN 9780228006596 (paper) | ISBN 9780228007302 (ePDF)
Subjects: LCSH: Iqbal, Muhammad, Sir, 1877–1938. Reconstruction of religious thought in Islam. | LCSH: Islam—20th century.
Classification: LCC BP161.I73 F35 2021 | DDC 297—dc23

This book was typeset in 10.5/13 Minion Pro.

Contents

Acknowledgments vii

Note on Translation and Transliteration ix

Introduction 3

1 Sir Syed's Representationalism 22

2 Knowledge, Experience, and Reality 43

3 The Cosmos as Self 68

4 The Human Being as Self 88

5 The Meaning of Revelation 103

Conclusion: Productive Tensions 118

Notes 123

Bibliography 153

Index 165

Acknowledgments

I am grateful for the support I have received throughout this project from teachers, family members, friends, and colleagues. This book builds on my doctoral work at the University of Virginia (UVA), in Charlottesville, where it was made possible by the intellectual demands and generosity of faculty and friends. I am utterly indebted to Peter Ochs for carefully nurturing my habits of thought. Peter Ochs, Shankar Nair, Ahmed H. al-Rahim, and Vanessa Ochs played a crucial role at UVA both in relation to my doctoral work and in helping me find my voice as a thinker and writer. I also owe an immeasurable debt to dialogue partners and friends I made through UVA, especially scholars associated with the Scripture, Interpretation, and Practice program and Scriptural Reasoning. They are far too many to name exhaustively, but include Kelly West Figueroa-Ray, Brian Siebeking, Emily Filler, Mark Randall James, Rebecca Epstein-Levi, Deborah Barer, Reuben Shank, Sara Aziz, Patrick Derdall, Omer Shaukat, Jacob Goodson, Susannah Ticciati, Randi Rashkover, and Nicholas Adams. Zain Moulvi's companionship and stamina for conversation were invaluable to this project.

My thanks also to colleagues at Lahore University of Management Sciences (LUMS University), especially Ali Usman Qasmi and Kamran Asdar Ali, who read through earlier drafts and gave helpful suggestions, and Ateeb Gul for his detailed feedback on transliteration.

In McGill-Queen's Studies in Modern Islamic Thought, the series editors, Humeira Iqtidar and Qasim Zaman, provided constructive comments and suggestions for the project. The feedback from the anonymous reviewers helped me make my arguments clearer and more hospitable to readers across different academic disciplines. The editorial team at McGill-Queen's University Press was immensely helpful. Richard Baggaley's counsel and Kathleen Fraser's prompt responses to my various questions eased the publication process. I am grateful to my copyeditor, John Parry, who was meticulous and thorough, and always available for conversation.

I am thankful to my parents, Asma Faiz and Faiz Bakhsh, and my brother, Usman, for their prayers and unwavering faith in me. I am also thankful to my parents-in-law, Rabia Nadir and Shahid Mirza, for their constant support. Finally, I would like to thank my wife, Zoya, who enriches and elevates every dimension of my being and whose love, patience, humour, and attention to detail sustain me daily. This book is dedicated to her and our daughters, Amani and Raavi.

Note on Translation and Transliteration

All translations, unless otherwise noted, are mine. All translations of the Qur'an are from Seyyed Hossein Nasr, ed., *The Study Quran: A New Translation and Commentary* (New York: HarperOne, 2015).

For all Urdu words and phrases, I have used the Urdu (in Arabic script) romanization table of the American Library Association – Library of Congress (ALA-LC). For all Arabic words and phrases, I have used the ALA-LC's Arabic romanization table. On occasion the same word has been transliterated differently depending on whether the original source was in Urdu or Arabic. For certain popular words and names I have followed their convenient and familiar anglicized versions – for example, Muhammad instead of Muḥammad, Qur'an instead of Qur'ān, Rumi instead of Rūmī and so on.

GOD, SCIENCE, AND SELF

Introduction

> He who used the magic of his pen to construct an Alexandrian wall to contain the flood of westernization, who was our defense against the global epidemic of secularism and irreligiosity, whose being sought to revolutionize our apathy into activity and struggle – he is no longer with us. The brightest lamp of our hopes has been snuffed by the cruel hands of death.[1]

These are the eulogistic terms in which Muhammad Iqbal (1877–1938) was remembered shortly after his death in a special "Iqbal issue" of the *Aligarh Magazine* dedicated to his life and work.[2] The themes expounded in that issue's essays and poems – philosophy, poetry, theology, politics, education, nationalism, the threat of secularism, the prospects of Muslim renewal (*tajdīd*) and reform (*iṣlāḥ*)[3] – encompass the wide range of Iqbal's legal, institutional, political, and literary activities. Iqbal was called to the bar at Lincoln's Inn, London, trained as a philosopher at Cambridge, obtained his PhD in Munich, worked as an educationist and instructor at different colleges in his adopted hometown of Lahore, sat in the Legislative Council of the Punjab Province of the British Empire, and was a Persian and Urdu poet widely acclaimed in his lifetime.[4]

As is the case with many prolific and popular scholars, the vast expanse of Iqbal's work as a poet, politician, activist, and public intellectual[5] has generated a multifaceted and contested legacy. In the intellectual and political landscape of colonial and post-colonial South Asia, "the last and greatest thinker of the historic 'Aligarh Movement'"[6] and arguably the most significant modernist Islamic thinker of the early twentieth century,[7] has been summoned as a sanctioning authority on both sides of any given contentious issue. Muslim separatists, Indian nationalists, socialist movements, dictatorial regimes, democratic politicians, Islamists and modernists – these are just a few of the varying and at times opposing camps that have invoked Iqbal's life and work to support their claims. Perhaps fittingly, then, Wilfred Cantwell Smith's survey of Islam in India discusses him in two sections: "Iqbal the Progressive" and "Iqbal the Reactionary."[8] Creation of the Iqbal Academy Pakistan, a federal statutory body, shortly after the partition of India in 1947 further proliferated and complicated his political and intellectual reception.[9] The academy has helped generate and sustain the field of "Iqbal Studies," with several universities in Pakistan offering programs on various facets of the life and work of the nation's poet-philosopher.[10] Within western academe, Iqbal's work has led to numerous conferences, edited volumes, monographs, and journal articles. Anthropologists, literary theorists, historians, religious studies scholars, political theorists, and philosophers have all grappled with Iqbal's body of work in an incredibly diverse range of projects.

Within the vast secondary literature generated on Iqbal's work, comparatively scant attention has gone to his philosophical magnum opus, *The Reconstruction of Religious Thought in Islam* (hereafter *The Reconstruction*), presented in the late 1920s as a series of lectures and then published in Lahore in 1930 and (with an added chapter) by Oxford University Press in 1934. In fact, Mustansir Mir, translator of Iqbal's verse and editor of Oxford's bibliography on Iqbal, notes that *The Reconstruction*'s philosophical content "still awaits a detailed study,"[11] roughly eighty years after its initial publication.[12] The limited scholarly study of its philosophical concerns mirrors the ambiguous and contradictory character of the reception of the rest of Iqbal's corpus. Heroic appraisals of the text label it "a promising glow" in modern Islam as it emerges out of the "dark background of the Middle Ages"[13] and declare it a successful synthesis of religion and science, sometimes leading to ecstatic pronouncements of its essential rootedness in "the epistemology of the Qur'an."[14] Alternately, dismissive appraisals describe the project as a metaphysical and devotional work, "occasionally merging into Islamic propaganda,"[15] "new wine into old bottles,"[16] as anachronistic apologetics that attempts to achieve the impossible, viz., framing and constructing relationships between discursive traditions (Islam and European science) that are essentially incommensurate.[17] More sophisticated critical-constructive appraisals offer varying assessments of Iqbal's approach and methods of re-envisioning Islam's scriptural resources in the context of colonial modernity. They tend to evaluate and modify the volume's attempts to "build bridges" between the pre-colonial intellectual heritage of Islam and discourses rooted in post-Enlightenment Europe.[18]

Despite their differences, these varyingly heroic, dismissive, and critical-constructive styles of receiving *The Reconstruction* acknowledge and concur that its plain sense is ambiguous, thematically eclectic, and philosophically perplexing. Some recent engagements with *The Reconstruction* attribute the work's ambiguous and troubled plain sense to the chaotic and crisis-ridden intellectual context of colonial modernity. Such analyses interrogate it as a project forged in the midst of and as a response to imperial modernity and its inauguration of the various "epistemological crises" that threatened the capacity of the Islamic intellectual tradition and scriptural resources to bear political ideals, ethical imagination, rationality, and truth.[19] They approach *The Reconstruction* as an attempt to engage critically with the political, social, institutional, and epistemological imaginaries of colonial modernity and embed it in an identifiable context with respect to which its claims acquire meaning. For instance, Hillier, using Alasdair MacIntyre's notion of epistemological crises, argues: "The epistemological crisis [that Iqbal grappled with] was the confrontation of Western modernity. Modernity (or Enlightenment) is its own distinctive intellectual-social-moral narrative histories . . . and when Modernity's values (e.g. anti-traditionalism, liberalism) conflicted with the dominant traditional values of . . . Islam, crisis ensued. Modernity's charge was that . . . Islam [is an] antiquated particularistic [tradition, which is] unable to participate in the modern world."[20]

The moral crises that Hillier and others refer to were propelled, in no small measure, by pedagogical environments such as Christian missionary schools and modern universities designed, in part, to rid the natives of India of their "superstitious" beliefs and "false" religions.[21] Iqbal was a graduate of the Scotch Mission School in Sialkot, studied at Government College Lahore, was an instructor of subjects including history, philosophy, and English at different colleges in Lahore, and, as such, fully implicated in the educational institutions of the British Raj. Muslim thinkers entangled in such pedagogical environments struggled with and reflected on the implications of European learning for the discursive resources of Islam. Many reflected especially on the concepts of religion, philosophy, science, revelation, and their possible inter-relations.

The Reconstruction of Religious Thought in Islam is Iqbal's most sustained philosophical discussion of these themes. The kind of recent scholarship to which I am referring attributes the confusions and cacophony of *The Reconstruction*'s philosophical mediation between the competing claims of the classical Islamic tradition and modernity to the epistemic upheavals germane to colonial modernity. Abdulkader Tayob, a contemporary scholar who thematizes Islamic discourse as it is crafted in relation to modernity, describes *The Reconstruction*, and Iqbal's work more generally, as a response to "modernity's challenges to traditional ideas of religion and culture."[22] Javed Majeed, in his introduction to the book's "American edition" of 2012 characterizes it as a philosophical exploration in which "Islam becomes an acute manifestation of the problems religions as a whole face in relation to modernity's processes of secularization and disenchantment and its 'scientism.'"[23]

A quick glance at how Iqbal created *The Reconstruction* lends credence to the sorts of observations Tayob and Majeed make about its problematic context. Iqbal formulated the book's philosophical concerns of mediating relationships between religion, scripture, science, and philosophy in a series of lectures delivered in 1929 at the invitation of the Madras Muslim Association. In 1925, the association had invited Sayyid Sulaimān Nadvī, a highly influential scholar and reformer, and a correspondent of Iqbal's, who spoke on the life of the Prophet. In 1927, Marmaduke Pickthall, a celebrated Qur'an translator and a founding editor of the journal *Islamic Culture*, delivered a lecture series titled "The Cultural Side of Islam."[24] Iqbal, in a "lecture-tour" during 1929, delivered the contents of *The Reconstruction* to the Madras Muslim Association, the Osmania University at Hyderabad, and finally to Aligarh Muslim University.[25] In 1930, and then in 1934, expanded to include a lecture that Iqbal delivered to the Aristotelian Society in London, what "many consider . . . the most important philosophical work of modern Islam"[26] was committed to print.

The public invitation to Iqbal's lectures in Madras gives a sense of the kind of audience he attracted. "These lectures," it reads, "are meant mainly for University students, undergraduates, graduates, and post-graduates and those, interested in the philosophical aspect of religion, are sure to derive immense profit and become acquainted with the history of religious thought in general and Muslim religious thought in particular."[27] Syed Zafarul Hasan, who was a professor of philosophy at Aligarh, presided over Iqbal's lectures there. In his closing address, Hasan remarked that Iqbal's philosophical work fulfilled an urgent need of modern Muslims by reconciling fraught relationships between religion, modern philosophy, and science. Hasan added that Iqbal had proposed routes to a "new theology" appropriate to the needs of contemporary Muslims.[28]

Iqbal's concerns surfaced in a review of his lectures by Marmaduke Pickthall, who delivered the Madras Muslim Association lectures in 1927.[29] He noted that the very difficult language and concepts of Iqbal's lectures probably "dazed and bewildered"[30] his audience and concluded that these lectures were "obviously designed to be read, and read most thoughtfully."[31] Pickthall remarks on the great service Iqbal performs for contemporary Islam by assisting Muslims who have fallen under the spell of "a certain mentality" shaped through "scientific education in a foreign medium."[32] The lectures address a confused "elite" for whom classical Islamic discourse can become meaningful only when it is juxtaposed with and communicated in terms of modern philosophical and scientific canons of thought. Iqbal's work challenges the "Pandits of modern thought,"[33] who imagine that religion is extraneous to modernity. Reflecting on the purposes of these lectures, Iqbal himself notes that their audience is Muslims who are shaped by western discourse, who "urgently demand" to understand Islam, philosophy, and science in commensurate terms.[34] Iqbal's "constructive" project consists in addressing the crises that ensue when the intellectual forces that shape and guide "Muslim youngmen" appear to be at war.[35]

The philosophical content of *The Reconstruction*, then, is situated and formed in an environment of epistemic crises. Recall, for instance, *Aligarh Magazine*'s portrayal of Iqbal as a bulwark against the "global epidemic of secularism" and the "flood of westernization." These crises threatened the capacity of Islam's intellectual and formative resources to bear meaning, rationality, and truth. In the face of modern[36] *Weltbilder* that emerge out of Newtonian, Cartesian, Lockean, Humean, Darwinian, and Freudian inquiries into the nature of reality, how could a community claim access to divinity and revelation?[37] All the more so if it asserts that the contents of a particular text were revealed in the form of speech at a particular moment in history to a particular individual, who embodies the perfect example for human conduct. How could modern Muslim subjects, formed through the educational institutions of colonial modernity, trust narratives and *Weltbilder* involving characters such as Prophets, a speaking God, and texts that are received as containing God's speech and communication to Prophets? In his correspondence with Iqbal, A.J. Wensinck, an editor of Brill's *Encyclopaedia of Islam*, sums up the crises and contradictions of modernity that Iqbal thematizes in *The Reconstruction*: "It seems to me that Islam is entering upon a crisis through which Christianity has been passing for more than a century. The great difficulty is how to *save the foundations of religion when many antiquated notions have to be given up*."[38]

"Modernist" Islamic discourse in colonial India – produced especially by thinkers participating in the educational institutions of the Raj – names a significant site animated by the perception that the discourses of colonial modernity imperilled the "foundations of religion" and demanded that "antiquated," pre-modern notions had "to be given up" in the light of those discourses. In this sense, *The Reconstruction* is an emblematic modernist text, anxious to discover habits of knowing that suit the knowledge claims of Islam's scriptural resources as well as modern scientific discourse. Its focus is articulating habits of thought that can nurture simultaneous commitment to the authority of scripture and the authority of experimental and observational investigation of social and natural reality.

Succinctly put, my case in this book is that *The Reconstruction*'s philosophical project of developing a rationality appropriate to religion, philosophy, and science is beset by two distinct tendencies of what it means to know something, which I label its "representational" and "pragmatic" voices. My argument is that the widely acknowledged, but misunderstood and under-theorized, equivocal, and confusing patterns of reasoning at play in *The Reconstruction* are traceable to these tendencies' co-presence in the text. On the one hand, the work's representational voice conceives knowledge as *descriptive*, *foundational*, *binary*, and *essential*. On the other hand, its pragmatic voice imagines knowledge as *performative*, *probabilistic*, *vague*, *and contextual*. I contend that referring the contradictions and confusions of the volume's theses about a rationality appropriate to religion, philosophy, and science to these two epistemological tendencies explains this text's complexities. In fact, I make a more precise claim: that the text's pragmatism – knowledge as performative, probabilistic, vague, and contextual – is Iqbal's attempt to refine and redress tendencies of knowing that place modernity in destructive competition with Islamic thought and practice. Its representationalism, I propose, is a *re-enactment* of the epistemological approaches that it criticizes.

Claims about the confusing, contradictory, or disjointed character of modern Islamic thought are fairly commonplace in scholarly and popular reflections on contemporary Islam. My interpretive work here models non-reductive ways of handling the ambiguities and inconsistencies of Islamic thought as it struggles to craft and discover novel ways for the Islamic intellectual tradition to bear truth and rationality in the context of modernity. But, more than that, I offer my readers a specific hermeneutical approach to re-reading what may appear to be intractably paradoxical, incongruous, or irrational elements of modern Islamic thought.

Through my reading of *The Reconstruction*, I show that modern Islamic texts that perceive their intellectual contexts to be crisis-ridden and attempt to correct them are fruitfully read as a dialogue, between their own re-enactment of what they criticize and possible ways of redressing the crises they are enmeshed in. Contemporary scholars have done a remarkable job of illuminating the aporias of modern Islamic thought by referring them to seismic shifts in the historical, political, and epistemological realities with respect to which modern Islamic thinkers articulate their work. My hermeneutical labour on *The Reconstruction* builds on and complements this scholarship. It does so by parsing out how the "crises of modernity" are enacted in the epistemological dynamics of philosophical thought generated in such moments of crisis.

For the rest of this Introduction I "unpack" the succinct account of my project that I've just given, starting with sketches of how I handle the features I have ascribed to *The Reconstruction*'s representational and pragmatic voices. The way these two epistemological tendencies shape *The Reconstruction*'s theses becomes clearer and less abstract during the course of this project. I ascribe four features each to the book's representational voice and its pragmatic voice.

The Reconstruction's representational voice shapes knowledge claims as *descriptive*, *foundational*, *binary*, and *essential*. The first feature – knowledge as *descriptive* – consists in supposing that the function of knowledge claims – whether religious, scientific, or philosophical – is to describe and represent already given objects and states of affairs. To make a knowledge claim is to utter a proposition, or to draw a picture, or to conceptualize an idea that mirrors or corresponds to what the proposition, picture, or idea is about.[39] A religious claim, then, is a report or description of a set of experiences or a state of affairs. Similarly, the task of science and philosophy is to develop propositions that describe reality. The media through which a claim is communicated, whether language, pictures, or any other semiotic form, function as "conduits" or "containers" that faithfully relay information about the objects of knowledge from one context to another.[40] The guiding norm for assessing the reliability of a claim is how much and how well it mirrors and represents what it refers to. This norm also entails that things are what they are, irrespective of their participation in processes of knowledge production. Or, in other words, that which a knowledge claim refers to is what it is, irrespective of its involvement in processes of reference. The function of a knowledge claim is to report data about things that do not get formed or affected by how they are reported on by such processes of description.[41]

The second representational feature – *foundationalism* – consists in thinking that the structure of knowledge is analogous to the structure of a "building"; that in order to construct knowledge claims, the knower must be able to specify and identify the propositions, ideas, or experiences on the basis of which they make knowledge claims. Any inquirer, in this view, must identify the "ground" on which they stand and articulate methods or processes whereby any other inquirer may be able to stand on the same ground. A hallmark of modern philosophy, foundationalism is analyzed by Susan Haack – one of its most notable commentators – as a two-sided commitment: namely, "(i) that some of our beliefs are epistemologically privileged (certain, indubitable, incorrigible or whatever) . . . and (ii) that any of our other beliefs that are justified, are justified by means of the support of these privileged beliefs."[42] Similarly, Richard Bernstein notes that foundationalism is akin to the pursuit of some sort of "Archimedean point" that serves as a "permanent, ahistorical matrix or framework to which we can ultimately appeal in determining the nature of rationality, knowledge, truth, reality, goodness, or rightness."[43] Such Archimedean points may be offered by thinkers in various forms: universally valid propositions, claims on behalf of "human reason," certain "basic facts" available to any and all possible inquiries, conceptual architecture that underpins all possible inquiry, or a set of experiences generically available to all human beings. The key: foundational claims are offered as infallible and available to any and all rational inquirers.

The third representational feature – *binarism* – is the assumption that, in any given universe, claims must be self-consistent and that contradictory claims cannot be attributed to the same object. Additionally, when *The Reconstruction* is being binarist, it analyzes different claims about a given object as divisible into two incompatible sets, one accurate and the other inaccurate. Peter Ochs, a theorist of the excesses of binary ways of organizing discourse, especially in religious and scriptural traditions, notes that "binarism" is the "tendency to overstate and over-generalize the usefulness of either/or distinctions . . . the inappropriate application of either-or distinctions to settings of irremediable ambiguity and probability."[44] When *The Reconstruction* is being binarist, it shapes its knowledge claims such that it can either make claim "S" or make claim "not S" about a given object of inquiry, and that all legitimate claims about the object must be either type "S" or type "not S."[45]

The combination of foundationalism and binarism – the second and third features of *The Reconstruction*'s representational voice – leads to the conclusion that resolving suspect claims, and the practices that have generated them, requires replacing them with novel claims that are treated as contradictories of the suspect claims. Religion or Science, Tradition or Modernity, Reason or Faith, Rationalism or Empiricism are instances of the application of an either-or logic to entire universes of discourse, which are divided into two sets and analyzed as contradictories.[46] The consequences of this combination of foundational and binary ways of shaping knowledge claims display themselves in *The Reconstruction* on several occasions.

The fourth feature – *essentialism* – conceives of the object of knowledge as composed of certain essential features that are global and timeless, along with other, inessential features, which are contingent and peripheral. It is to assume that certain features of the object of knowledge are primary and basic, and others are secondary and derivative. Thus, inquiry seeks the substantial or essential features of its object. This "core" is predicated as being universal and permanent, whereas the "husk" represents contingent, time-specific, and less interesting features. As you may notice, there is a certain kinship between essentialist and foundational ways of organizing knowledge claims about an object. An epistemological approach that seeks permanent and timeless foundations for knowledge is isomorphic with one that conceives the object of knowledge itself as composed of certain essential and timeless features. Tayob in his study of Iqbal and the Islamic reformer Sir Syed Ahmed Khan (1817–1898) notes that this way of conceptualizing religion and Islam is germane to their work. He postulates that modernists predicated a core to the object of their interest, viz. Islam, as a strategy to gather a sense of stability and a "foothold" in a world that otherwise appeared to them chaotic and senseless.[47]

In conclusion, these inter-related features of reasoning about knowledge, its relationship with its object, and the agent of knowledge permeate

The Reconstruction's argumentation. When Iqbal speaks in a representational voice, he attempts to secure the capacity of religious claims to bear rationality and truth by arguing that both pre-modern religious claims and modern science represent reality in identical ways. He displays his representationalism, for instance, when he claims that proper introspection, carried out by any given human being, will inevitably reveal that selfhood (*khudi*) is the most basic category for interpreting the universe; or that, during Islam's history, a "Magian crust" has formed over its "original core."[48]

The four features of what I have labelled *The Reconstruction*'s "pragmatic" voice correspond to the ones I have identified above in its representational voice. Its pragmatic voice takes knowledge claims as *performative, probabilistic, vague, and contextual.*

First, conceiving knowledge as *performative* sets up knowledge claims to diagnose and correct the practices in which those claims are situated. This feature of Iqbal's pragmatic voice takes knowledge claims as the performance and outcome of a process of inquiry stimulated by some question in the inquirer's environment.[49] Their function is to guide and regulate practices of inquiry seeking to address some problem in a particular context of knowing. In this view, knowledge claims provide hypotheses as well as courses of thought and action to address the issues that the makers of those claims have identified.[50] Claims are verified by their capacity to resolve the problems that afflict a context of knowing, rather than their capacity to accurately mirror or correspond to a given state of affairs.[51] Claims' meaning is displayed in the habits of practice of some community, and inquiry aims to redress the problematic practices in which it is situated. A quick way to summarize the performative aspect of Iqbal's pragmatic voice is that it conceives knowledge claims as instruments of problem solving and assesses them in terms of their capacity to resolve problems.[52]

Second, *The Reconstruction*'s pragmatic knowledge claims appear in *probabilistic* terms. Consider, for example, claims about the outcome of a football match or the weather. Such claims are justified by evidence and arguments that can be modified, debated, and rejected. They are made about situations and objects that are not fully certain, determined, or complete. Similarly, when speaking probabilistically about an idea or an event, Iqbal admits that it may obtain in some situations and fail to obtain in others. He refrains from all-or-nothing claims and shapes his claims in corrigible terms. His probabilistic claims are offered as hypotheses, justified by revisable warrants, rather than infallible judgments, premised on unassailable insights.[53]

Third, Iqbal's pragmatic tendency admits that certain objects of knowledge are *vague*. Such objects are appropriately handled by claims that are probabilistic, inconsistent, and contradictory, rather than self-consistent.[54] Consider an example Peter Kang uses to highlight a vague situation where inconsistent claims are appropriate. He notes that the claim "Everyone either loves me or hates me" is an either-or claim employed in a situation that is not handled adequately in either-or terms.[55] My relationships with people constitute a situation where inconsistent predicates are applicable: some people may love *and* hate me. They are also the kinds of situation where the different ways people relate with me are not adequately analyzed as *either* forms of love *or* forms of hate. People may be indifferent to me, admire me, be envious of me, think me childish, or polite, or rude. Predicates that are relevant or applicable to my relationships with people may not be self-consistent and may not be adequately handled as divisible into two sets, one of which is true at the expense of the other.[56] Daniel Weiss, in a recent study of Herman Cohen's articulation of concepts that are appropriate to religion, argues that communicative inconsistencies and rational contradictions that inform Cohen's concepts are not a "sign of faulty reasoning," but Cohen's way of addressing the paradoxical character of the objects of his inquiry.[57] Similarly, Shahab Ahmed, as he articulates a conceptual vocabulary to deal with the vast expanse of Islamic history, develops the notion of "coherent contradictions."[58] Ahmed and Weiss contend that such concepts need to be developed in order to handle phenomena such as "Islamic history" or "Jewish thought." Such phenomena require inquirers to develop a form of discourse that can handle vagueness rather than flattening it according to the strictures of a rationality that rejects contradiction as fundamentally irrational.

Fourth, when speaking pragmatically, *The Reconstruction* marks its knowledge claims by their *contexts*. A contextual claim is "triadic" or "three-part": it consists of the claim itself (1), what the claim is about (2), and the processes through which it is developed (3). In this view, it makes little sense to speak of a knowledge claim "as such"; a claim emerges out of specific methods, norms, and practices of investigation. It makes sense, can be debated over, verified, polished, rejected with respect to some process of inquiry, in which it has its life. Contextual claims are not "dyadic" or "two-part." Claims (1) are not about something (2) generically. They are about something by way of some process of inquiry (3); inquiries are finitely organized, and even abstract claims relate to some investigative procedure. That a particular claim is general or abstract is a function of its applicability or relevance to a large or perhaps even indefinite domain of reference; its generalizability does not "free" it from the processes of inquiry out of which it emerges.

When teaching this aspect of Iqbal's pragmatic voice in classrooms, where students become anxious of the "relativistic" consequences of contextual thought, I often cite the way Nicholas Adams distinguishes between contextual and non-contextual claims. He notes that contextual claims tend to gesture towards some aspect of their originating environment and processes. Non-contextual claims leave their environments unstated and tend to invite over-generalizations. Both types of claims are concerned with questions of truth, verification, and reliability, but engage in such processes in different ways.[59]

These set of features comprise *The Reconstruction*'s pragmatic voice of configuring knowledge. They are on display, for instance, when Iqbal argues that concepts are instruments that help an organism navigate its complex environments; when he claims that conceptions about Islam have to account for the presence of unity and diversity, permanence and change, in its history; when he argues that the human self is immortal and free; and when he develops relationships between the concepts of knowledge, experience, and reality.[60]

Before I offer snapshots of the following chapters of this study, I would like to clarify my reading of the relationship between what I hypothesize and label as Iqbal's representationalism and his pragmatism. I proposed above that Iqbal's representational voice re-enacts the kinds of epistemological approaches to religion, philosophy, and science that he criticizes and finds problematic. His pragmatic voice offers potential ways of addressing the epistemological problems that *The Reconstruction* identifies and is situated in. But I don't want to give my readers the impression that Iqbal's representational and pragmatic voices are simply denials of each other. His pragmatic epistemological voice is not a rejection of his representational epistemological voice but an *attempted repair* of it. Consider each of the features I have isolated in his two voices. The pragmatic features do not reject but rather modify the representational features: from descriptive to performative; foundational to probabilistic; binary to vague; essential to contextual.

Performative claims do not dispense with descriptive claims altogether but modify the relationships between descriptions and the objects they are about. Conceptualizing knowledge claims as performative does not do away with propositions or pictures or diagrammatic tools more broadly in conceptualizing an object. Performative claims re-order descriptions as accounts of how to conduct specific practices of inquiry. The health of a descriptive claim, in this view, is judged by how well it can organize, guide, modify, or maintain some practice of inquiry. Briefly put, a performative approach reads descriptive claims as implicit or explicit instructions for guiding a practice of inquiry rather than as claims that mirror reality as such.[61]

Similarly, a probabilistic approach does not deny that, in any given practice of inquiry, certain claims function a-critically and indubitably. But it does not treat such claims as unassailable and epistemically privileged foundations for the architecture of knowledge. Iqbal's probabilistic approach re-reads foundational claims as revisable hypotheses that fund a given practice of inquiry.

In the same vein, admitting that some objects are vague does not dispense with binary claims. It simply means that not all possible objects and situations can be expressed in binary terms. Binary claims are appropriate and indispensable in any setting where claims such as "pass the salt" (not the pepper) or "the cup is on the table" (not on the floor) are being uttered and exchanged. Admitting vagueness is not denying the applicability and efficacy of binary claims in such situations, but only admitting that *certain* situations call for a discourse that admits probability, inconsistency, and contradiction. As we saw above, Weiss and Shahab Ahmed's work demonstrates that phenomena such as "Jewish thought" and "Islamic intellectual history" cannot be appropriately handled in binary terms.[62]

And, lastly, a contextual approach reconfigures claims about "essences" to claims about "mind-independent" features of an object of inquiry. Iqbal's contextualist approach does not imagine that objects of inquiry are reducible to the inquirer's constructions and that, apart from their participation in processes of inquiry, objects have no "mind-independent" existence or being of their own. Instead, it asserts that mind-independent phenomena become accessible to us in connection with some specifiable investigative procedure. Iqbal's contextualist approach concedes that there are things out there in the world that are independent of what we may think about them. But our knowledge claims about such objects are *not* independent of the specific modes of analysis we bring to bear on such objects; mind-independent things become accessible and knowable through methodologically specific inquiries.[63]

The Reconstruction's pragmatic voice, in this reading, corrects the way representational epistemologies configure relationships between religion, philosophy, and science. The text's *own* representational tendencies, I propose, are vestiges and marks of its struggle to modify and correct the excesses of these tendencies. The co-presence of representational and pragmatic voices in *The Reconstruction* speaks to Iqbal's unresolved attempt to repair his epistemological context. But, as I say this, I don't mean that his book – or other texts of Islamic thought entangled in crisis-ridden epistemological contexts – should *ideally* be resolved and consistent. Or that it, or other confusing and troubled texts of modern Islamic thought, fail to measure up to the canons of resolved and self-consistent thought. I contend that texts that perceive their epistemological environments to be grave threats to the traditions of thought and practice whence they emerge are *appropriately* and *rationally* unresolved. A "pitch-perfect" mode of argumentation by a text that also shrieks at the crises it is addressing should, in fact, make readers suspect the intensity of those crises.

Here's another way of stating what I mean: If *The Reconstruction*'s theses about the relationship between religion, philosophy, and science were strictly representational, they would be consistent, not perplexing and confusing. But then Iqbal would have been simply re-enacting the epistemological norms he criticizes. If his book's theses were fully pragmatic, they would have been consistent, too. But this would have cast doubt on Iqbal's claims of being engulfed in serious epistemological problems, since no mark or evidence of such problems would have been visible in his own thinking. What I label *The Reconstruction*'s "representationalism" consists of tendencies of knowing Iqbal criticizes as a moribund path for relating religion, science, and philosophy. What I label its "pragmatism" is a way to correct the epistemological norms Iqbal criticizes. His text practices what it criticizes, because, although it challenges the epistemological norms it is enmeshed in, and offers ways to address the epistemological problems it takes up, it is crafted amidst those same norms. The wounds or scars of *The Reconstruction*'s struggles with representationalism are visible in its own representational tendencies. I've labelled this process of re-enacting and redressing the problems a text criticizes "attempted repair." The theses generated by trying to fix a problematic context are confusing, because they contain corrections as well as the errors they seek to fix. Since repair is attempted amidst a problematic context, reparative thought is marked by the problems with which it wrestles.

In the chapters that follow, I use this interpretive approach to clarify how the two epistemological tendencies I've identified in *The Reconstruction* drive its perplexing patterns of reasoning. We also witness the different degrees to which Iqbal's attempted repair resolves specific issues.

In chapter 1, I begin to isolate and clarify the pragmatic and representational tendencies of *The Reconstruction* by analyzing a prototype of a consistent display of representationalism. My purpose is to illustrate the modernist tendencies of knowing that *The Reconstruction* inherits as it tries to correct them. For my prototype, I have chosen to analyze the innovative and path-breaking exegetical essays on the Qur'an by Sir Syed Ahmed Khan, "founder" of the Aligarh Movement, and arguably the most significant late-nineteenth-century modernist thinker of colonial India.[64] While the works of any number of Indian Muslim modernists may serve as fine examples of the epistemological tendencies that inform Iqbal's intellectual habitus, Sir Syed's œuvre is uniquely suited to my present purposes. Apart from the fact that Sir Syed is widely recognized as perhaps the most influential Indian Muslim modernist,[65] two warrants inform my choice.

First, considerable evidence links Iqbal's modernist conceptualizations with Sir Syed's religious thought. For instance, Tayob notes that Iqbal's philosophical reflections on religion, Islam, and their meaning in modernity are fruitfully read as "successors" to Sir Syed's thematization of these issues.[66] In his correspondence with Sahibzada Aftab Ahmad Khan, a vice-chancellor of the Aligarh Muslim University, on issues pertaining to reforming Islamic theological thought, Iqbal acknowledges Sir Syed as a "prophetic" pioneer whose work needs to be built on and improved.[67] Riffat Hassan identifies Iqbal as the "greatest thinker of the historic 'Aligarh Movement'" initiated by Sir Syed.[68] Javed Majeed contends that *The Reconstruction* builds on and transforms Sir Syed's scriptural hermeneutics and conceptualizations of Islam.[69] My concern, however, is not to establish some form of unquestionable historical continuity between these two figures.[70] My point is that, since *The Reconstruction* was published in English, and delivered in the form of lectures across various Muslim universities, including Aligarh, Iqbal is offering it to Muslims whose intellectual habitus was shaped in no small measure by Sir Syed's modernist concerns and epistemology. This makes him an effective avenue for elucidating the epistemological tendencies that shaped the intellectual context Iqbal sought to repair.[71]

Second, while *The Reconstruction* may be read fruitfully against other contexts of inquiry or by identifying other features of its problematic context – there is a whole host of works titled "Iqbal and X" – I look at Sir Syed here to present a clear and consistent model of the representational tendencies in *The Reconstruction*, which Sir Syed's religious thought more fully and consistently embodies. Chapter 1 is intended to, first, isolate Iqbal's representational tendencies from his pragmatic tendencies in order to diagnose the confusions that mark *The Reconstruction*'s arguments and, second, to help me display how the latter is an attempt to repair the former.

Chapter 2 does two things. First, it focuses on how *The Reconstruction* employs the concepts of knowledge, experience, and reality as it argues that religion, like science and philosophy, offers distinct modes of inquiring into human experience. I show how Iqbal uses these terms to address regnant approaches in his context that deem religion epistemologically empty and privilege philosophy and science as modes of inquiring into the meaning of human experience. Second, it shows how *The Reconstruction*, when it works through the idea of religious experience, violates the epistemological norms it sets up when it mediates the concepts of knowledge, experience, and reality. My purpose here is to indicate how the confusions in Iqbal's case for the epistemic value of religion and religious experience emerge because *The Reconstruction* co-performs pragmatic and representational tendencies of knowing. The chapter shows that Iqbal corrects foundationalist and essentialist approaches to religion but does not adhere to his own corrections in his discussions of particular religious traditions.

Chapters 3 and 4 take up the "master category" of Iqbal's philosophical thought, viz., the category of selfhood (*khudi*).[72] My analysis in chapter 3 is two-fold. First, I discuss selfhood's various functions in *The Reconstruction* and then focus on its central role in conceptualizing relations between religion and science – namely, to build a framework that pulls together knowledge claims from "revelatory" and "experimental" contexts of inquiry. Second, I consider how Iqbal argues that various sciences (physics, biology, psychology) relate their practitioners with God's self. Iqbal criticizes accounts of scientific knowledge that take it as some sort of unmediated disclosure of reality, corrects them by discussing physics and biology as performative and corrigible enterprises, but then takes psychological introspection as a path to unmediated disclosures of reality. Iqbal's pragmatic corrections of scientific knowledge claims are meant to counteract the tendency to read discourses from different contexts as mutually exclusive, while his own reading of psychology enacts the kind of exclusivist style he criticizes.

Chapter 4 examines Iqbal's conceptualization of human persons as selves. Human selfhood (*khudi*) is a significant site in *The Reconstruction* where Iqbal is most consistently pragmatic in his analyses. He criticizes approaches that attribute global and timeless features to the human person and positions that take subjectivity to be an epiphenomenon, decomposable to more basic and primary things. After navigating anthropologies that Iqbal criticizes, I discuss his own procedures for conceptualizing the human person: a three-pronged style that is cenoscopic, probabilistic, and aspirational. I concentrate on how this style is at play as Iqbal attributes freedom and immortality to human beings. His pragmatically corrected conception of human personhood exemplifies how different anthropologies can be articulated by a particular tradition of thought and practice without rendering such difference oppositional.

Chapter 5 examines *The Reconstruction*'s philosophical exploration of how revelatory experience and scriptural claims may acquire significance, meaning, and referentiality. I start by examining how *The Reconstruction* attributes features to Islam and Muslim culture in three broad forms. First, Iqbal offers his claims as binary, combative descriptions of the "spirit of Islam," in competition with other, contemporary descriptions; second, he presents non-binary, formulations that admit contradiction; and, finally, he submits his claims as attempts to transform the rules of attributing features to Islam operative in his context. Iqbal criticizes approaches that delegitimate Islam by conceiving biological and psychological disorders as the "core" of revelatory claims. He corrects such approaches by arguing that Islam ought to be conceptualized as a complex phenomenon that is "in the making" and displayed in the lives of Muslims. He repeats the errors he criticizes by positing an authentic "core" of Islam, which is concealed by Muslims who adhere to the "Magian crust" that has historically formed over this core.

The second part of chapter 5 examines *The Reconstruction*'s scriptural hermeneutics. It shows that Iqbal tends to read scriptural claims in two ways. First, he reads them as descriptive propositions, whose meaning is secured by their correspondence to a given state of affairs. Second, he reads them contextually, as claims whose meanings are displayed with respect to some habit of interpretation. Iqbal discusses scriptural meaning as observable in the habits of interpretation and activities of those who engage with scriptural texts, but he also reads these texts for underwriting non-contextual, essentialist descriptions of reality.

I would like to give my readers a few clarifications and express some of my hopes about this project before presenting my substantive arguments in the following chapters. The first thing I'd like to clarify is that I'm not claiming that scholars err when they ascribe confusion to *The Reconstruction*'s theses about religion, philosophy, and science and that if one knew "how to read it right" its confusions would disappear. I am trusting scholars who describe *The Reconstruction* – or other works of modern Islamic thought – as confusing and seek to explain their confusions in the light of extensive shifts in the historical and political realities in which modern Islamic thinkers articulate their work. This book supplements such scholarship by hypothesizing that a significant source of *The Reconstruction*'s confusing theses about religion, philosophy, and science is the conceptions of knowing operative in the text. I intend my substantive arguments to lend credence to the idea that *The Reconstruction* corrects and repeats the epistemological norms it criticizes.

I also hope that my hypothesis – that modernist Islamic texts repeat and correct what they criticize – may offer a way to interpret confusing theses about religion, philosophy, and science advanced in other such texts. A less modest hope is that my hermeneutical approach might offer a way to handle the complexities and confusions of philosophical texts that present high-pitched assessments of their own problematic contexts and crises. My work models an approach for reading such texts as a dialogue between their re-enactment of what they criticize and possible ways of redressing the crises in which they are enmeshed.

In the service of my overall aim of displaying the epistemic norms at play in *The Reconstruction*, I am not taking up this influential work for the sake of "placing" it in Iqbal's complete œuvre.[73] Discussions about its "place" in Iqbal's corpus assume several shapes. Some scholars read it as a remarkable Urdu and Persian poet's disappointing attempt at philosophizing.[74] Others read it and Iqbal's poetry as commensurate and inter-related forms of discourse.[75] Still others argue that Iqbal's poetic work should not be discussed in the same breath as or for the sake of excavating his philosophical outlook.[76] I am eschewing such debates about genre and classification because my purpose is not to give my readers a sense of how to classify *The Reconstruction* as an element or part of a "great thinker's" corpus.

Rather, my project discusses *The Reconstruction* as a valorized but under-theorized work of modern Islamic thought. As Mustansir Mir notes, there has not been a single sustained study on the philosophical theses of what is widely acknowledged as one of the central texts of modern Islamic thought since its publication in 1934. My approach to *The Reconstruction* in this volume aims to fill this major lacuna.[77]

What sort of yardstick might one use to judge the health of my hermeneutical work on *The Reconstruction*? I would like to offer two such criteria, which I put forward also as avenues of future collaboration, debate, and productive disagreement between my readers and me. The first is the degree to which my claims resolve the perplexities of the book's readers in the face of its theses about religion, philosophy, and science. I am, above all, keen to hypothesize and spell out the epistemic sources of those confusions.[78]

The second criterion is the degree to which my hypotheses about *The Reconstruction* help readers generate their own philosophical and hermeneutical expositions of confusing theses advanced in other modern Islamic texts. To be sure, I'm not suggesting that the specific epistemic voices I've located in Iqbal simply echo throughout modern or modernist Islamic thought. The ambiguities, complexities, and contradictions of other such works may, of course, be unique to them. My work argues, through a specific case, that such confusions and contradictions are the visible wounds of the struggle between such thought's re-performance of the errors it names in the world and the possible remedies it provides.

I offer one last clarification. My entire project is composed of hermeneutical strategies with which I engage *The Reconstruction*. During this process, I rely *functionally* on analytical vocabularies developed by semioticians, Islamicists, philosophers, and theologians.[79] I refer to different analytical vocabularies strictly to illustrate and elucidate particular hermeneutical moves I make to expose the two epistemological voices that, I hypothesize, drive *The Reconstruction*'s theses. As scholars from different disciplines engage with this book, I invite them to complicate, challenge, and observe my hermeneutical work in the illustrative light of analytical vocabularies they find valuable in their various disciplines.

CHAPTER ONE

Sir Syed's Representationalism

Sir Syed Ahmed Khan (1817–1898)[1] – educationist, essayist, and knighted functionary of the judicial apparatus of the British Empire in colonial India – is a central figure in nineteenth-century Muslim approaches to relating pre-modern Islamic intellectual traditions with the "new sciences" (*ʿulūm-i jadīdah*). One of the elemental features of Sir Syed's "modernism"[2] is that religious claims, to be sound, have to be commensurate with scientific claims. In this chapter I clarify how Sir Syed renders religious and scientific claims commensurate with each other by working through his exegetical writings on the Qur'an that reflect on religion, scripture, and science.

My purpose is to reveal the features of knowing that inform Sir Syed's project of re-describing and recovering the capacity of religious claims to express truth in the context of colonial modernity. Sir Syed argues that religious claims, when they function well, adequately describe, like other knowledge claims, the objects they are about. He recovers their capacity to describe their referents adequately by identifying the husk of ill-conceived beliefs and practices (viz., trusting in miracles, believing in the supernatural, anthropomorphizing nature) that unfortunately inform "historical" Islam. He then isolates this "husk" from the "kernel" of Islam, which accords with God's intentions, faithfully conveying and describing the beliefs of Muhammad and his companions.[3]

Sir Syed develops a foundational principle of interpreting Islam's scriptural resources to access this kernel. His principle of interpretation creates insurmountable division between his own intellectual practice and the practices of inquiry he inherits. The truthfulness of his excavation of the meaning of Islam's scriptural resources entails that, in the history of qur'anic interpretation, other meanings attributed to the verses he reads are errant and false. As he conceives it, his task is to construct and perform an intellectual practice that addresses the cognitive ills affecting Muslim reasoning practices vis-à-vis religion, scripture, and science in colonial India.

The epistemological side of Sir Syed's intellectual practice – exemplified in his innovative exegetical work on the Qur'an – is a consistent prototype of what this book calls "representationalism." In this chapter, I intend to exhibit the various ways Sir Syed's project of harmonizing religion and science takes knowledge as descriptive, foundational, binary, and essential. My point is two-fold: to exemplify a consistent representational epistemology in relation to Islam's scriptural resources and to give my readers an illustration of the epistemological environment in which Iqbal's masterwork, *The Reconstruction*, renders religion, philosophy, and science commensurable.

The argument in this chapter is divided in two sections. In the first I discuss Sir Syed's principles of exegesis and the conceptions of religion, scripture, science, and their inter-relations embedded in those principles. In the second I examine specific passages from Sir Syed's exegetical work on the Qur'an to show his principles in action. I also give examples of his attempt to structure non-antagonistic relationships between claims that emerge from different and seemingly incongruous sources. I show how his exegesis delivers a discursive universe in which the claims of pre-modern scriptural texts and those of the new sciences can cohere because they describe reality in similar, identical, or non-contradictory terms. I conclude by summarizing how Sir Syed's project of articulating religious thought anew is representational. It is funded by a *foundational* principle of interpreting the Qur'an that allows him to uncover the *essential* meaning of qur'anic verses, which accurately *describe* the true referents of the Qur'an and pit him in *binary* conflict with other reception histories of the Qur'an.

I

In 1892 Sir Syed published a tract (*Taḥrīr Fī Uṣūl al-Tafsīr*), where he clearly lists and discusses the exegetical principles he employed in his engagement with the Qur'an during the previous two decades.[4] The work consists of three parts: a prefatory comment, a series of letters exchanged between him and his close associate, Syed Mehdi Ali,[5] in 1892, and a list of fifteen principles on which he bases his engagement with the Qur'an.

Sir Syed's prefatory comment situates his exegetical work on the Qur'an in a narrative context that locates him both within the history of the British Empire in India and in Islamic intellectual history more broadly. He writes that after the mutiny (*g͟hadr*) of 1857 – a complicated "revolt" against the British East India Company, involving disgruntled sepoys, the queen regent of Oudh, the Mughal emperor, and various factions of the north Indian elite – he was moved to reflect on and reform (*iṣlāḥ*) his community.[6] He concluded that India's Muslims could not meaningfully address the crises they were undergoing unless "they [learnt] those new arts and sciences (*'ulūm o funūn-i jadīdah*) that are the source of pride of other communities, and to learn them in the language [i.e., English] that reigns supreme – by God's will – in our land."[7]

In order to fulfil this aim he set up a society for translating scientific and historical texts from English into Urdu and, among other things, established one of the first modern Muslim colleges in Aligarh.[8] His literary and institutional endeavours were conducted in an environment where the new sciences were viewed with suspicion because of a particular assessment: "It was apparent that whoever excels in these [new] sciences (*'ulūm*) – whether Christians, Muslims, or Hindus – ends up bidding farewell to their religious beliefs (*maẕhabī 'aqā'id*). [Those who engage with] the new sciences deem the conclusions of these sciences to be true and accurate and when they find that their religious beliefs are contrary to the new sciences, they judge them to be false."[9]

Sir Syed accordingly decided to inquire into the validity of such commonly held views by examining exegetical (*tafsīr*) works on the Qur'an. His initial research was quite disappointing; he finds that such texts are filled, almost without exception, with spurious, inaccurate, and mythical content. "[Given the state of *tafsīr* literature] I began, to the limit of my capacities, to reflect on the Qur'an in order to understand the principles on which its structure (*naẓm*) rested. And, to the limit of my capacities, I found that according to the principles on which it rests, nothing in it or in Islam is contradictory to the new sciences."[10]

Sir Syed next reproduces his correspondence with Mehdi Ali that prompted him to formalize his principles of interpretation. This exchange is initiated by Mehdi Ali, who is perturbed after reading some of Sir Syed's exegetical work on the qur'anic narratives of "miracles" performed by Jesus and Moses in their prophetic careers, as well as his exegesis of the *jinn*. What unsettles him is Sir Syed's claim that the qur'anic text does not affirm Jesus' miracles or the existence of angels and the *jinn*:[11]

> I am saddened that you have taken up opinions (*masā'il*) that educated Europeans nowadays – those who are not fully religious in either belief or practice – believe to be true, certain, and unobjectionable. And have read the verses of the Qur'an [in accordance with those opinions in such a way that] even the word independent interpretation (*tāvīl*) does not do justice [to the eisegetical character of your work]. You heartily curse Muslim exegetes and refer to them as blind imitators of Jewish scholars. But you, yourself, have reposed your trust in the non-religious thinkers of this age [and have interpreted the Qur'an according to their stances] . . . Neither the context of the verses, nor the words of the Qur'an, nor the idiomatic conventions of the Arabs support your claims.[12]

In fact, according to Mehdi Ali, Sir Syed's reading of the Qur'an would not satisfy or please God.[13]

In his reply, Sir Syed thanks Mehdi Ali for his confrontational rather than devotional reading of his exegetical work.[14] Where Mehdi contends that his exegesis is contrary to God's purposes, Sir Syed replies that the prejudices of his upbringing blind him. Mehdi Ali's clinging to the fantastic tales he was told as a child makes him susceptible to trusting the scholars (*'ulamā*) and the exegetes (*mufassirīn*), whose work appears to him as the disclosure of God's purposes.[15] It is not Sir Syed but Mehdi who is misguided because he trusts the eisegetical impositions of the exegetes on the Qur'an, over Sir Syed's more reliable commentary. He pleads with Mehdi Ali to not receive "the religion of Islam as stories about fairies and demons."[16]

Mehdi Ali's next, extremely detailed and caustic retort is worth recounting. It spurs Sir Syed to elucidate his principles of exegesis and illustrates the epistemologically problematic environment that stimulated Sir Syed's modernist concern to render religion and the new sciences commensurable. Mehdi Ali begins by stating that he prefers to stay "entrapped in the quick-sand of received doxa,"[17] rather than, like Sir Syed, attempting to build relations between religion and the new sciences. Following Sir Syed would mean risking "descent into a deep, dark cave, filled with fire."[18] Sir Syed may think him childish for believing in miracles, or the existence of angels, and the *jinn*, but the proponents of the new sciences would likely ridicule Sir Syed and his attempt to make peace between scientific and scriptural claims:

> My dear [Sir Syed]! You have accused me of not understanding the elevated character of your exegesis because of my adherence to the stories I was fed as a child, which stories have damaged my capacities of thought and reflection. But tell me – if the philosophers and scientists of this age who . . . are spreading a new light in the world – if they say about you that even though you [Sir Syed] have given up imitation of your ancestors, think their books are rubbish (*raddī*), make fun of (*taẓḥīk*) the scholars and exegetes . . . but – despite your elevated reason, enlightened consciousness, investigative thought, wise mind – are *still* entrapped by the tales you were told as a child . . . and continue to believe in God and Prophets [How shall you respond to them?] I do not mean to insult you but . . . the philosophers . . . and practitioners of the new sciences say exactly this about people who hold religious ideas.[19]

Mehdi Ali then launches a volley of remarks that further challenge the notion that the sciences of their time could make peace with the discursive resources of Islam: "A God who creates . . . listens, knows . . . is wise," how can someone who thinks on the pattern of Hegel and Darwin affirm such a being?[20] If there is a God that Darwin and Hegel affirm, it is not the God of Abraham and Muhammad but a mere "first cause."[21]

Mehdi Ali's letter culminates in a hail of pronouncements: "Modern science has issued its fatwa: God's existence is suspended . . . Prayer and worship are a product of the fear and anxiety of ignorant and unrefined people. Prophethood is a veil of deception. Revelation (*vaḥī*) is a myth. Inspiration (*ilhām*) is a dream. The soul is perishable. The Day of Judgment is a hoax. Reward and punishment are human fantasies. Heaven and hell are meaningless words. Human beings are merely advanced apes."[22] How can Mehdi Ali's "revered Sir Syed, [his] beloved master (*murshid*),"[23] begin to think that rapprochement is possible between the new sciences – whose conclusions are clearly anathema to notions of God, prophecy, scripture – and Islam?

Sir Syed begins his response by remarking on his correspondent's scattered and panicked critique. Sir Syed can rectify their haphazard and scattered debate by outlining the principles he has employed in his exegetical work. If Mehdi Ali agrees with them, his concerns about Sir

Syed's interpretation of prophetic miracles, angels, and the *jinn* will be allayed and their disagreements will be resolved.

The narrative context in which Sir Syed situates his principles of exegesis begins to display the features of knowing that inform his overall project. Confronted by a divisive environment that pits religion against science, Sir Syed's proposed healing of this environment sets up a corresponding antagonism between his exegetical practice and the practices of qur'anic interpretation he inherits, which he sees as beset with problems that are beyond correction. This tradition has forsaken what he takes to be its primary task: viz., describing the way the Qur'an was received and interpreted during the Prophet's lifetime. It has, instead, laced the text with unreliable, sometimes pre-Islamic Arabian, at others pre-Islamic Jewish and Christian myths.

The conflict between the new sciences, which are a reliable means of investigating nature,[24] and the scriptural resources of Islam has come about because the latter have been approached through erroneous patterns. These patterns may have seemed reasonable at an early stage in both human history as well as the history of the Muslim community. But the various improvements in human knowledge, exemplified by the new sciences, demand that these old patterns, along with the foundations on which they rest, be discarded and replaced.

Sir Syed's judgment that he has inherited a practice, E_1, that is irrevocably errant sunders his discursive universe into two: the errant practice of exegesis (*tafsīr*) on the one hand and a potential, constructed practice of exegesis, E_2, on the other. E_1 and E_2 are contradictory; E_1 is errant, E_2 is not-errant. Sir Syed's E_2 is accurate or true at the expense of the E_1 he inherits. This is identical to the pattern through which Mehdi Ali, and Sir Syed's contemporaries, envision the relationship between religion and science. As Mehdi Ali puts it, *either* religious claims about reality are true and there is a God, Prophets communicate with God, there is life after death, and so on. *Or* scientific claims about reality, contradictories of such claims, are true.

Sir Syed's project of mending relations between religion and science relocates the pattern of opposition between them to the practice of exegesis he inherits (E_1) and his constructed practice of exegesis (E_2). Only a new pattern of interpreting the Qur'an can mend the division between religion and science. As you can see, Sir Syed's wholesale critique of the tradition of practice that he wishes to repair through his own contributions sets up a contest governed by the law of excluded middle; either he or the classical and medieval exegetes are trustworthy or accurate interpreters of the Qur'an. This is an epistemological environment that I've labelled "binarism":[25] A typical feature of a binarist claim is the extension of a particular predicate ("is erroneous") beyond a specifiable and contextualizable referent to a non-contextualized and general referent such as "the exegetical tradition." Insofar as the most significant distinction between the criticized E_1 and the constructed E_2 is that one is in error and the other isn't, the differences between the two practices become oppositions.

In fact, Sir Syed takes the form in which his practice intervenes in the area of qur'anic interpretation to be a display of a formal feature of how knowledge functions and "builds" on antecedent practices. For him, the accumulation of knowledge by a community of reasoners and inquirers in any given field of inquiry is marked by severe disruptions – for example, the transition from Ptolemaic to Copernican astronomy, from Aristotelian to Newtonian physics. In such moments the foundational assumptions of a particular epistemic environment (*zamānah*) are discarded and replaced by surer, more trustworthy foundations. In an essay titled "The New Sciences" (*'Ulūm-i Jadīdah*), Sir Syed notes that the transition from Greek sciences to modern, European sciences saw newer basic principles replace the basic principles (*uṣūl*) of the previous sciences.[26] In "The Progress of Knowledge" (*Taraqqī-yi 'Ulūm*), he notes: "The errors of Greek science are openly visible, and [in its place] the new sciences stand on excellent and secure foundations (*mustaḥkam bunyād*)."[27] As the foundations of knowledge claims become more secure, they are also able to represent reality more accurately. For example, the Greek sciences, with what we now know are faulty foundations, imagined the sun revolved around a stationary earth. Modern science describes the sun's motion in relation to the earth more accurately partly because its foundations are truer to reality. For Sir Syed, then, the accumulation of knowledge is a historically extended, continuously ruptured process, which, as it unfolds, represents reality progressively more accurately.

Sir Syed's reworking of the exegetical tradition imagines that the traditions or practices of reasoning that an actor or a community inherits are akin to a building.[28] This "building," during the course of the history of the community that is "housed" in it, may continue to serve its needs with minor "repairs" and the addition of rooms here and there. But, with the passage of time, its inhabitants will discover that its foundations are in fact flawed. In such moments of crisis, it would be incumbent upon those reasoners who have detected fundamental flaws in their community's inherited structures of reasoning to demolish the flawed building and to furnish novel, better, more secure foundations for new and sustainable practices of reasoning.[29] Epochs are distinguishable partly by their different – and progressively more accurate – "grounding" knowledge claims. Given Sir Syed's conception of knowledge, members of the same community who belong to different epistemological epochs or regimes, grounded by different epistemological assumptions and foundational claims, struggle interminably with each other to form accurate representations of reality.

The kinds of doubts the new sciences pose about religion – summed up in Mehdi Ali's recounting of their "fatwas" on religion – demand new foundations for interpretive relations with scripture. Sir Syed offers his principles of interpretation to this end. In fact, as we observed above, he claims that the principles he seeks to articulate are identical to those that ground the entire composition (*naẓm*) of the Qur'an.[30] This way of constructing the relationship between the object of one's inquiry and one's claims about it suggests that in order to interrogate one's object (in this case the Qur'an) adequately the inquirer is to imagine that one's object of inquiry – like the practices that examine it – is akin to a building. The foundations of the house of knowledge are secure and trustworthy to the degree that they are identical to the foundations on which the subject matter of knowledge rests.

Sir Syed concludes his 1892 statement of his exegetical principles by listing fifteen such principles. His overarching purpose here is to convince Mehdi Ali and his audience more generally that a) his exegetical concern of disproving miraculous and supernatural readings of the Qur'an and b) his concern of proving that the Qur'an's claims are congruous with the claims of western philosophy and science rest on sound, qur'anic principles. His most prominent principle to this end is that "nothing in the Qur'an contradicts the law of nature,"[31] which he treats as synonymous with the phrase, "the work of God and the word of God cannot contradict each other."[32] Whereas "word of God" (*varḍ āf Gāḍ*) is one of his synonyms for the Qur'an, we see the imprecision of his conception of creation in his many, synonymous terms for "work of God" (*vark āf Gāḍ*): for example, nature (*fiṭrat*),[33] creation (*makh̲lūqāt-i ʿālam*),[34] existents (*maṣnūʿāt-i ʿālam*),[35] law of nature (*qānūn-i qudrat*),[36] laws of nature (*qavānīn-i qudrat*),[37] the work of God (*Kh̲udā kā kām*),[38] and the habits of God (*ʿādat Allāh*).[39] Both Sir Syed's contemporaries, such as Ali Bakhsh,[40] and later scholars – for example, Christian Troll – criticize his unclear deployment of these terms. Troll criticizes the "lack of precision" of Sir Syed's usage of these terms and notes that he "neglects to define them clearly when he uses them."[41]

Rather than taking Sir Syed's imprecise descriptions of the work of God or creation or the law of nature as a problem that can be rectified by a clear definition, or an occasion to clarify his muddled thinking, I take his opacity as a symptomatic feature of his conception of nature and creation. Sir Syed has widely been described as a naturalist and a deist who imports reigning notions of nature and the "book of nature" from nineteenth-century deistic theology, as they were being articulated in Britain and elsewhere, into Islamic thought. According to Barbara Metcalf, for instance, "In his scheme God was a Deist First Cause, a remote impersonal God who did no more than set in motion laws that then worked themselves."[42] Similarly, Dietrich Reetz remarks that Sir Syed "followed a deist concept when he equated the Work and Word of God. [He is like] Voltaire and Rousseau who supposed God had simply set the clockwork of the universe going."[43]

If Sir Syed is to be described as a "naturalist," which his opponents use as an epithet to discredit him, as well as being a label he reclaims for himself, we must specify how his conception of creation or existence is "naturalistic" and not view his position as purely derivative of naturalistic Enlightenment thought. In fact, Sir Syed wrote an essay to dispel the idea that his conception of creation or "the work of God" is deistic.[44] In this essay, he voices his critics' concerns in the following terms: if God has created the world according to certain patterns, does this not effectively absolve (*ma'zūl, mu'aṭṭal*) God from the functioning of creation?[45] Just as the operation (*caltī*) of a watch is not related to its builder, does Sir Syed's position not entail that creation continues to function independent of its creator?[46] In response to such lines of criticism, he notes that God's relationship with the world is not comparable to a watchmaker's with the watch. Nor is the functioning of a watch comparable to that of the universe. God's activity, which is the cause of all being, is not comparable to a watchmaker's, who is the cause of a particular being, i.e., a watch. While a watch may be "self-sustaining" after it has left its constructor, the patterns that operate in the universe do not possess any agency or capacity to sustain their own activity. God is the ground and source that sustains (*qā'im*) the continual functioning of creation. As the perpetual sustainer and regulator of creation, "God is never out of work."[47] Contrary to Metcalf's assertion that Sir Syed believes that the universe works according to self-sustaining patterns and Reetz's that he models the universe as a "clockwork," he himself denies that the universe, by virtue of being rule-bound, is self-sustaining.[48]

A close inspection of what he means by the "work of God" or "creation" or "the laws of nature" suggests that Sir Syed is committed to the formal principle that nature or creation is patterned and ultimately transparent to human cognition. Creation is characterized by rules and regularities susceptible to reflection, manipulation, and investigation; nothing in creation or nature is ontologically mysterious or unamenable to rational analysis, and the patterns that constitute the course of nature are ultimately ascertainable.[49] This formal commitment does not mean that Sir Syed is also committed to a fully ascertained or given body of knowledge about such rules or patterns: "It is true that we are not aware of all the laws according to which nature operates. In fact, we are aware of very few laws and our knowledge of even those laws is incomplete (*nāqiṣ*) and not absolutely definite (*pūrā*)."[50]

The formal character of Sir Syed's commitment to the regularities that constitute the course of nature is evidenced in his essay "The Reality of Miracles" (*Muʿjizah Kī Ḥaqīqat*), which recommends a three-step process to investigate a strange, mysterious, or inexplicable event (*ʿajīb vāqiʿah*):[51]

- Gather evidence (documentary, perceptual, etc.) that confirms the occurrence of the inexplicable event.
- See if the data of your investigation can be explained and comprehended by means of the current understanding of the course of nature.
- If the previous step fails, rest assured and accept that the inexplicable event is amenable to human cognition and that it occurred according to regularities or processes of nature of which we are currently unaware.

The point is that the incomprehensibility of strange or unpatterned events is a function of the investigator's ignorance and the epistemological environment they are a part of. The patterns governing nature or creation are always operative and never suspended or violated. Sir Syed grounds the inviolability of the course of nature as he discusses his principles of exegesis through various scriptural verses, such as Q 54:49, 30:30, and 33:62. He reads verses such as 33:62 ("and you will find no alteration in the wont of God") as propositional descriptions of the inviolable character of the patterns that constitute creation. The inviolability of the course of nature constitutes an operational covenant (*'amalī va'dah*) God abides by;[52] any unregulated, miraculous event that contravenes the course of nature (*k̲h̲arq-i 'ādat*) would make a liar out of God. In fact, if God had inserted human beings in a created order with intrinsically mysterious features, that would have been akin to God appointing a cow or a donkey as a magistrate in a city.[53]

Sir Syed's overall position is that the knowledge claims of any inquiry refer to the work of God, i.e., one or another facet of creation. The history of human thought, punctured by foundational disruptions, is one of incrementally describing creation more adequately. The new sciences are (merely) one stage, albeit the most improved and advanced stage so far, of describing creation accurately. Similarly, scriptural interpretation, which is an inquiry comparable to other fields of investigation into creation, makes knowledge claims about God's word or the Qur'an. Sir Syed's central principle of exegesis, then, is that methodologically sound investigation of God's speech and God's work generates mutually commensurate knowledge claims.

But what is progress in the investigation of scripture? How does Sir Syed's work improve on his predecessors? Akin to the new sciences in relation to creation, his exegetical writings "overturn" assumptions about scriptural claims and the logics for approaching them. His exegetical principles look to provide novel and more appropriate foundations for interpreting Islam's scriptural texts. Their purpose is to displace ancient and erroneous principles that have informed the "mainstream" of the exegetical tradition. He argues that his exegetical principles and particular knowledge claims – for instance, that the Qur'an does not affirm the existence of miracles, angelic beings, or the *jinn* – more accurately represents its utterer's purposes and that his claims accord with Muhammad and his companions' reception of the Qur'an.[54]

By overturning mainstream exegesis, Sir Syed is recovering crucial elements of the Qur'an's "original" reception, which were obfuscated during Islam's history. Epochs after him, he argues, will be able to clarify and describe the Qur'an's original reception and its utterer's intentions even more fully and accurately. What actually happened as the Qur'an was interpreted and received during Muhammad's life serves as Sir Syed's frame of inquiry, and he anticipates that future scholarship is likely to improve on and, if need be, overturn his own work.[55] As he carries out his task, he imagines two potential "charges" against his position: first, anachronistic reading, and second, "turning the Qur'an into a toy in the hands"[56] of its readers.

As for the first charge, he claims that, despite his novel interpretive claims, he relies on readings potentially available to the Qur'an's original readers. The linguistic conventions of Arabic, idiomatic usages, and grammatical rules that governed the speech of Islamic and pre-Islamic Arabs protect Sir Syed from attributing anachronistic meanings to the Qur'an.[57] Even if Sir Syed's interpretive conclusions are absent from, or were marginalized, in the Qur'an's reception history, this does not render his interpretive work anachronistic:

> [As I show that the Qur'an does not refer to miracles or anthropomorphic beings] some of my brethren will get angered and [will adduce evidence to show] that the Qur'an contains references to 'un-natural' miracles. [I shall reply politely,] 'The verses you present as proof of un-natural miracles in the Qur'an: is it possible to read them differently – remaining true to the linguistic and literary conventions of the Arabs and idioms and metaphors of the Qur'an?' [If such interpretations are possible, I shall rest my case.] . . . If they reply by asserting that during the thirteen centuries of Islam neither the companions of Muhammad, nor their successors, nor the successors of the successors, nor the exegetes set forth the meanings you have determined . . . we shall respond politely: 'Spare us this argument and tell us if the meanings we have determined are in keeping with the words, idioms, metaphors of the Qur'an.'[58]

While mainstream exegetes may disagree with Sir Syed, his claim is that the principles of his inquiry are well-suited to the Qur'an's original reception, crucial elements of which may have so far escaped the traditions of its reception. His task is to describe meanings, as they were intended by God, and received in the context of the Qur'an's revelation and production. The original "core" of the Qur'an's reception is likely to become clearer with the passage of time as historians, theologians, exegetes, and lexicographers approach the text with better evidence, and sounder, more reliable, foundations of inquiry. The task of critical, contemporary exegesis is to gather evidence in order to pierce through and go behind the reception histories of the Qur'an to discover its original reception. As long as there is evidence to support the claim that a given interpretive reading was available to the original audience of the

Qur'an's reception, the novelty of Sir Syed's interpretive claims does not make them anachronistic.

The second charge of Sir Syed's interlocutors – "turning the Qur'an into a toy in the hands" of its readers – builds on the first. It contends that interpreting the Qur'an according to epistemological assumptions that are foundationally ruptured during the course of the Muslim community's history makes a mockery of the holy text. As we saw above, Sir Syed imagines that acquiring knowledge is a foundationally grounded project. While it is under way certain moments require replacing old foundations with newer ones, to secure a more accurate vision of the object of knowledge, which Sir Syed labels variously "creation," "nature," and so on. Consequently, different epistemological epochs are in interminable competition with each other, with each successive era securing more accurate relations with nature or creation. If such fundamental discontinuities ought to be germane to the reception history of the Qur'an, too, as Sir Syed contends and performs through his work, how can the communities of its reception maintain that the Qur'an is truth-bearing? Sir Syed articulates this charge as follows:

> It is said to us sarcastically: 'When Greek wisdom, astronomy, and philosophy spread among Muslims, then considered accurate and in accordance with reality, the scholars of Islam affirmed portions of the Qur'an that seemed in agreement with those sciences, and tried to make commensurate with those sciences those portions (of the Qur'an) that appeared contrary to them. Today when it is known that those sciences were built on wrong first-principles, that their astronomy was absolutely opposed to reality, and when natural sciences have made more progress, you [Sir Syed] contradict those meanings which earlier scholars determined according to Greek sciences and adopt other meanings which agree with the sciences of the present day. It will be no wonder if in the future these sciences advance further and the things which today appear fully ascertained may be proven wrong. The need will arise of establishing other meanings of the words of the Qur'an and so on. So the Qur'an will become a toy in the hands of its readers.[59]

Sir Syed responds that any advance in the natural sciences belies only previous *interpretations* of the Qur'an and leaves intact its capacity to represent truth: "As the sciences continue to advance and as we ponder over it [i.e., the Qur'an] with regard to these advanced sciences, it will become known that its words are in agreement with reality in the light of these (newer sciences too), and it will be proved to us that the meanings we determined earlier, and which were proved wrong now, were a fault of our knowledge, and not of the words of the Qur'an."[60]

Sir Syed addresses this response not just to Mehdi Ali and his interlocutors. He is likely gesturing towards his own life history. In 1848 he wrote a tract defending a geocentric, Ptolemaic view of a stationary earth around which the sun revolves. He offered this as a cosmological doctrine that had to be defended against the "teaching of the new sciences [being taught] in the Government colleges of Agra, Benares, and Delhi."[61] By the 1870s, when he starts penning his exegetical essays on the Qur'an, he becomes an advocate of a heliocentric view, argues vehemently against his former self, and asserts that the Qur'an does not contradict such a position: "Let us say that we understood from the Qur'an that the Sun revolves around the Earth," he writes to Mehdi Ali, "and now we learn that the Sun is stationary and the Earth revolves around the Sun."[62] In such a situation, if we turn to the Qur'an again, Sir Syed avers that we will learn that our geocentric reading of the Qur'an was our interpretive mistake, not a conclusion necessitated by the text.[63]

By reading the Qur'an such that it can potentially accord with both a geocentric and a heliocentric conception of the solar system, Sir Syed disburdens the text from any given picture of the cosmos while burdening it with a formal claim. That is, the Qur'an has the plasticity to remain commensurate with the representational capacities of any established practices of knowing. It will be readable such that its contents will not contradict the progressively improving representations of nature or creation.

What is more, such reading, while belying previous traditions of reading, is likely to shed light on and illuminate features of the Qur'an's original reception.[64] Just as creation is not belied when we discover that our representations of it are faulty (i.e., geocentrism), so the Qur'an is not contravened when we discover that the history of its reception rests on flawed foundations. In fact, for Sir Syed, it is the fate not of the Qur'an, but of its investigators, that is on the line in any engagement with the text: they will be proven (fundamentally) wrong about the word of God over and over again, much as creation's investigators have been about God's work time and again. Just as the latter are richer and truer for discarding geocentrism for heliocentrism, for adopting Newton's physics over Ptolemy's, for choosing evolutionary over non-evolutionary models of biology; in the same way, studies of the Qur'an will benefit through Sir Syed and others after him who will overturn his work and radically revise the terms of historical, lexical, theological, and hermeneutical scholarship on the Qur'an.[65]

II

Sir Syed's exegesis of the *jinn* and the "miracles" of Moses and Jesus illustrates how he puts into practice the exegetical principle that nothing in the Qur'an contradicts the course of nature. He uses a combination of three strategies for tackling apparent references in the Qur'an to anthropomorphic beings and miraculous events. First, he argues that such references are a retention and a report about pre-Islamic Arabs' beliefs in such phenomena. Second, for expressions such as "angels" (*malā'ikah*) and "*jinn*," he finds textual warrants for a non-miraculous reading as historically, lexically, and idiomatically viable. Third, for seemingly inexplicable events, he offers an explanation based on relatively stable hypotheses offered by the sciences of his time.

Using the first strategy for terms such as angels (*malā'ikah*) and *jinn*, he finds textual warrants to show that these seemingly supernatural verses refer to the "erroneous and absurd" (*ghalaṭ aur behūdah*) beliefs of pre-Islamic Arabs.[66] This strategy builds on his distinction between purposive (*kalām maqṣūd*) and merely instrumental (*kalām ghair maqṣūd*) text or speech. Sir Syed notes that an interpreter's basic challenge in relation to the Qur'an, and texts more generally, is determining the purposes and intentions of the utterer of the text or speech (*kalām maqṣūd*). This is no simple task, since texts and utterances rely on expressions and devices (*kalām ghair maqṣūd*) that say nothing about the utterer's intentions, and are subordinate to the utterance's larger purposes. Identifying expressions that serve as mere vehicles for conveying the actual meaning of the text is a significant hermeneutical challenge. The Qur'an is replete with expressions that are employed purely instrumentally by God:

> In determining the meanings of the Qur'an we must settle whether the speech upon which we found our argumentation is the real end of what is said (*kalām maqṣūd*) or just the means of the speech (*ghair maqṣūd*). For if it is the latter then argumentation cannot be based upon it. 'Not end' speech (*kalām ghair maqṣūd*) is found in

> the Qur'an in many places and in human speech too it occurs . . . For example God says, 'Verily, those who say our signs are lies and are too big with pride for them, for these the doors of heaven shall not be opened and they shall not enter Paradise until a camel shall pass into a needle's eye' . . . From this one cannot argue that at some time in the future a camel will pass through the hole of a needle, because this is not the intention of what is said. It is meant to express the impossibility of the entry of those people into Paradise who belied God's signs. Likewise one cannot argue upon this verse that heaven has doors, for these words are not said with that intent, but are intended to express the idea that they will be deprived of God's mercy.[67]

Furthermore, the Qur'an contains expressions that retain how Muhammad's Jewish, Christian, and polytheistic contemporaries employed them. The Qur'an refers to elements of the social world in which it was revealed, but this does not mean that it endorses the reality of such elements.[68] The Qur'an may refer to *jinn* and magic, without affirming the existence of anthropomorphic beings or supernatural events.[69] The notion that the universe is populated by *jinn*, by powerful, invisible beings, created of smokeless fire, who can shift their appearances and perform fantastic feats, is a vestige of the "erroneous and absurd" beliefs of pre-Islamic Arabs, a product of their speculation and imagination.[70] The Qur'an may retain, mention, or refer to such "erroneous beliefs" and fantastic beings without affirming their reality.[71]

Sir Syed deploys his second strategy – attributing a non-miraculous meaning to a seemingly miraculous phenomenon – in relation to the word *jinn* in the Qur'an by commenting that the word's semantic field allows it to mean something "hidden" or "concealed," a usage he shows to be prevalent at the time the Qur'an was revealed. He then argues that the word's real referents are wild and unruly (*vaḥshī*) human beings who live in mountains, jungles, and desolate (*vīrān*) areas, concealed and hidden away from cities.[72] When the Qur'an uses the expression *jinn*, it refers either to the fanciful ideas that a particular group of people believed in or to wild and uncivilized human beings, living beyond the settled populations in Arabia. In either case the Qur'an is not referring to any mysterious entities.[73]

Sir Syed also applies the second strategy to interpret seemingly miraculous attributions to Jesus in the Qur'an. For instance, about part of Q 3:49 ("I [i.e., Jesus] will heal the blind and the leper and give life to the dead by God's Leave"), he notes that many scholars see Jesus as a miracle-worker because they uncritically accept Jewish and Christian traditions of interpretation: "It is a chief habit of the scholars of Islam that they subject the meaning of the Qur'an to the traditions of Jews and Christians and that is why they have interpreted [the Qur'an] to mean that Jesus used to make blind people see and heal lepers and quicken the dead."[74] Sir Syed is not dismissing Christian and Jewish scriptures as unreliable and corrupt – he believes that those texts, in their current form, are loci of divine revelation. He argues rather that reading the Gospels with a historical and critical lens (*tārīkẖānah taḥ qīq*) shows that the attribution of miracles to Jesus is a *misreading* of the Gospels.[75]

In the light of the epistemological epoch that Sir Syed belongs to and helps usher in, the errors of the commentators of Jewish and Christian scriptures are parallel to those of Muslim interpreters of the Qur'an. The Qur'an's (and the New Testament's) intended meaning in stating that Jesus healed people with leprosy and blindness is that he restored people with physical disabilities from the margins of society and made them rightful members of the kingdom of God (*Ḵẖudā kī bādshāhat*). Jesus proclaimed that God's mercy is accessible to all, irrespective of physical appearance and capacities, and this constitutes "healing" the sick.[76] Similarly, when Q 3:49 mentions that Jesus gave life to the dead, it is a reference to how Jesus rescued people from spiritual death: "A human being's spiritual death is being a disbeliever. Jesus, by proclaiming God's oneness and by communicating God's commandments, was raising people from the death of disbelief (*kufr kī maut*)."[77]

Sir Syed's third strategy – explaining an apparently miraculous event using relatively stable hypotheses offered by the *'ulūm* or sciences of his time – is on display in his reading of the miracles Moses performed at the pharaoh's court. We can see this strategy at work vis-à-vis Q 7:107–8: "So he [Moses] cast his staff and, behold, it was a serpent manifest (*thu'bān mubīn*). And he drew forth his hand, and behold, it was white to the onlookers (*nāẓirīn*)." Sir Syed begins with a relatively stable hypothesis of the sciences of his time – namely, staffs do not suddenly turn into serpents and hands do not suddenly turn white. He then offers lexical evidence that this verse necessitates no such sudden transformations. The verse states that Moses' hand *appeared* white to the onlookers and that his staff only *manifestly* (or *visibly*) became a serpent.[78] The exegetical question then becomes: how is it that a hand can appear white all of a sudden or how can a staff appear as a serpent? And Sir Syed relies on the sciences of his time to explicate this situation: "Every human being, whether prophets, or friends of God (*auliyā*) or ordinary human-beings, belonging to any religion – in fact, even animals – have a power of magnetism (*quvvat-i maqnāṭīsī*) which causes effects on the being itself [human or otherwise] and those around it."[79]

Human beings have the capacity to mesmerize people into seeing things that are not there and experiencing events that do not actually occur. Such an ability is a perfectly natural, explicable phenomenon.[80] The practitioners of mesmerism have always been with us. The difference, today, says Sir Syed, is that a whole scientific discipline has developed that scrutinizes and studies this phenomenon. Sir Syed is referring to the science of mesmerism, named after Franz Anton Mesmer, an eighteenth-century physician. Its purpose was to study, quantify, and make therapeutic use of capacities whereby human beings can affect the demeanour and states of consciousness of other human beings.[81] Moses, then, was performing no extra-ordinary or supernatural feat and was making use of his mesmerizing capacities that are generic to the human species.[82]

Sir Syed uses all three strategies to show that the Qur'an's contents measure up to the epistemological canons of his era. In fact, he avers that his canons of interpretation, forged in the fire of an advanced episteme, free of the clutches of ancient practices of knowing (*qadīm ʿulūm*), have helped clarify to contemporary Muslims that Muhammad and the early Muslim community did not believe in miracles or *jinn*-like creatures. To the degree that the Qur'an appears to make such claims, it is only accurately describing the mistaken beliefs of the pre-Islamic Arabs. Similarly, Moses exercised a perfectly explicable human capacity of mesmerism. He may not have been aware of the underlying science, but what he practised was regular and patterned, and more crucially, the Qur'an retains the patterned and explicable character of the events that unfolded at the pharaoh's court.

Sir Syed's exegetical practice is grounded by a foundational principle of interpreting the Qur'an – viz., the work of God does not contradict the word of God. This principle allows him to uncover the core meaning of qur'anic verses, which has been obfuscated during the text's reception history. The core meanings Sir Syed discovers consists of propositions that accurately describe the true referents of qur'anic verses. The descriptions that he uncovers – for example, that Muhammad and his companions did not believe in beings such as angels and *jinn* or that Moses practised the art of mesmerism in the pharaoh's court – are consistent with the claims of the new sciences and place him in binary conflict with other reception histories of the Qur'an. His exegetical practice is a consistent illustration of a representational epistemology (i.e., knowledge as descriptive, foundational, binary, and essential) brought to bear on the relationship between religion and science. I've detailed his representational approach with two main purposes in mind: to give my readers a prototype of the epistemological practices that *The Reconstruction* is forged in and addresses and to prime them to observe the various guises of representationalism in *The Reconstruction* as an object of criticism as well as the engine of some of the book's arguments about religion, science, and their inter-relation. This chapter seeks to help readers distinguish Iqbal's criticism and construction of representational arguments from his pragmatic corrections of such arguments.

I am going now to examine a signature symptom of representationalist ways of relating religion and science. The pattern is visible in Sir Syed's hermeneutical approach to the Qur'an and appears regularly in *The Reconstruction* as a symptom of its representationally constructed arguments. In Sir Syed's hermeneutics, this pattern is displayed in the following way: he mends the conflict between religion and science and, in the process, relocates this conflict to another domain of reference. In the process of "making peace" between religion and science,[83] he generates unresolvable conflict between his constructed practice of exegesis, E_2, and the practice of exegesis, E_1, that he inherits.

Peter Ochs offers a set of formal strategies for detecting hermeneutical practices that generate conflict in their attempt to make peace and labels such practices a "hermeneutics of war."[84] I'm going to burden my readers with a technical account of Ochs's formal strategies because a "hermeneutics of war" is a major symptom of *The Reconstruction*'s representationally constructed arguments.

Ochs suggests a four-stage method to detect if this pattern is at play:

- A thinker identifies a set of problems in a given practice (E_1) and narrates those problems using a set of descriptive propositions.
- They propose solving these problems with another practice that they construct or promote (E_2) and narrate the solution, E_2, using a set of descriptive propositions.
- They argue that E_1 and E_2 are incompatible practices, i.e., one can adopt either but not both.

- They argue that the universe of all possible practices is exhausted by E_1 and E_2.[85]

According to Sir Syed, his inherited practice of exegesis (E_1) inaccurately displays how the Qur'an was interpreted and received during Muhammad's lifetime. The practice he promotes (E_2) can accurately describe the Qur'an's interpretation and reception during that era and, he contends, address the seemingly intractable conflict between religion and science. His attempt to modify his contemporaries' interpretation of religion, scripture, and science in a bid to show that both religion and science are truth-bearing re-enacts the hermeneutics of war:

- Religious claims, R_1, and scientific claims, S_1, appear to conflict.
- R_1 is a product of specific practices of interpretation, E_1, in relation to the Qur'an.
- S_1 is a product of practices of interpretation I_1, in relation to nature.
- There is evidence that I_1 is accurate.
- The conflict between R_1 and S_1, coupled with the accuracy of I_1, suggests that E_1 is errant.
- A new set of interpretive practices, E_2, is needed to replace the errant practice E_1.
- Applying E_2 to the Qur'an leads to religious claims R_2.
- E_2 is non-errant because R_2 does not conflict with scientific claims S_1.
- Since R_2 and S_1 are not in conflict with each other, E_2 and I_1 are reliable practices of interpretation.
- Thus interpretive relations with both nature and the Qur'an are truth-bearing.

Sir Syed recommends applying this procedure whenever tensions arise between the sciences interpreting nature and those interpreting scripture. As we saw above, in doing so, Sir Syed pictures the acquisition of knowledge as a progressively more accurate means of describing the object of knowledge, propelled by increasingly more secure foundations for knowledge claims. Interminable conflict between epistemological environments with different foundations is a structural feature of knowledge acquisition. Please note the pattern enacted in Sir Syed's harmonization between religion and science: he mends the relationship between the problematic pair of religion and science and, in the process, relocates this conflict to another domain of reference. In the following chapters, the epistemological norms of his rapprochement between religion and science, along with the pattern I've just noted, recur, in different guises, as easily identifiable markers of Iqbal's representational voice.

CHAPTER TWO

Knowledge, Experience, and Reality

The Reconstruction is deeply animated by the kinds of questions that course through the exchange between Mehdi Ali and Sir Syed we explored in chapter 1. How may a community claim access to divinity and revelation in the face of *Weltbilder* emerging out of Newtonian, Cartesian, Lockean, Humean, Darwinian, and Freudian inquiries into the nature of reality? Iqbal is just as wary as Mehdi Ali of the new sciences' implications for communities whose worlds involve narratives and characters such as a speaking God, scriptures, prophets, and theodicean teleology. Iqbal laments that the modern age, with its "tyranny of imperialism," is not just a political arrangement whereby western powers have subjugated and established their dominion over "weaker peoples."[1] Imperial modernity elementally transforms how colonized subjects know, perform, and express their relationships with the world.[2]

For Iqbal, the institutional and discursive instruments of imperial modernity rob colonized subjects "of their religions, their morals, of their cultural traditions and their literatures."[3] He summarizes the hazardous implications of modern thought under the label of "atheistic materialism" and judges its ethico-political and epistemic consequences to be "the greatest danger to modern humanity."[4] Politically, in Faisal Devji's analysis of Iqbal's critique of colonial modernity, "atheistic materialism" is generative of territorially bound nationalisms, spurred by the "race-idea," producing a political order that has "destroyed or at the very least enfeebled all ethical or idealistic imperatives in political life, making for an international regime of parochial and so continuously warring interests."[5] Such political life takes flight, in Iqbal's reckoning, on the wings of a metaphysical dualism that confines religion to subjectivity, to a "matter of private opinion," by carving out an objective public order, unhampered by religious ideals.[6]

On its epistemological side, for Iqbal, as for other Muslim modernists, modern modes of knowing are most threatening in their silencing of Islam's scriptural resources, incapacitating them from bearing rationality and truth. In Wensinck's words, the "great difficulty" that confronts modern Islamic intellectual culture, and its institutions and actors, "is how to save the foundations of religion when many antiquated notions have to be given up."[7]

Sir Syed attempts to follow the path that Wensinck imagines for religious traditions such as Christianity and Islam: forsaking "antiquated notions" in order to save the "foundations" of these religions. As chapter 1 showed us, Sir Syed rescues Islamic discourse from the threats enumerated by Mehdi Ali through a particular model of knowing. In building commensurate relations between religion and modern thought, he negates the reliability of any earlier practice of knowing in scriptural and scientific discourse. For Sir Syed, contemporary Muslims need not be "shackled" by their institutional and intellectual history, except for the historical situation in which the Qur'an was revealed to the Prophet.

In contrast, when Iqbal thinks about the relationship between contemporary Muslims and their past, he notes: "We should not forget that life is not change, pure and simple. It has within it elements of conservation also . . . Life moves with the weight of its own past on its back . . . In any view of social change the value and function of the forces of conservatism cannot be lost sight of . . . No people can afford to reject their past entirely."[8] The "revision of old institutions" is a "delicate" task, wherein the "responsibility of the reformer"[9] is grave; reformist tendencies can err in conceiving stasis or "conservatism" as an oppositional force to avoid, rather than one to combine with "dynamism" in reform activities.[10]

As I noted in chapter 1, the representational dynamic in Sir Syed's reformist hermeneutics is a prototypical illustration of intellectual responses to the perceived crises of modernity that Iqbal's *Reconstruction* addresses. In a letter to one of his friends where he discusses the prospect of translating his "Reconstruction" lectures of 1929 from English into Urdu, Iqbal writes: "The audience (*mukhāṭib*) of these lectures consists of mostly those Muslims who are shaped by western philosophy and who desire that Islamic philosophy should be articulated (*bayān*) in the language of modern philosophy. [The book's intended audience is Muslims who desire that] if there are shortcomings in [Islamic philosophy], these shortcomings should be addressed. My work is mostly constructive (*ta'mīrī*)."[11]

This chapter explores *The Reconstruction*'s philosophical conception of religion, such that religion or religious claims are not reduced to "antiquated notions." It examines how Iqbal's conceptualization of religion is marked by the representationalist approaches he criticizes as well as by his attempts to correct them. My argument is divided in three sections. The first takes us through *The Reconstruction*'s use of the categories of "knowledge, "experience," and "reality."[12] I show that Iqbal employs these categories to argue that "religion" names an environment where knowledge claims about the meaning of human experience are constructed, exchanged, and debated. I also offer a reading strategy for clarifying how these terms relate with each other in the text. The chapter's second section reveals how Iqbal's contextual approach to knowledge shapes his conception of religion and its relationship with science. In the third section I show how some of *The Reconstruction*'s arguments about religion run afoul of its contextual approach to knowledge and become instead foundational, binary, and essentialist. This third section makes clear how *The Reconstruction* reiterates the epistemological practices that it criticizes.

The chapter argues two points. First, the concepts of knowledge, experience, reality, and religion operate inconsistently in *The Reconstruction.* Second, the confusing and inconsistent use of these terms in the text is a function of its representational and pragmatic voices.

I

The first chapter of *The Reconstruction* sets up a conceptual theatre that presents the categories of knowledge, experience, and reality in relation to claims about religion, philosophy, poetry, and science.[13] The chapter title –"Knowledge and Religious Experience" – is not straightforward; a plain-sense reading could suggest, for instance, that Iqbal is going to make major distinctions between knowledge and experience in the first chapter of his book. And, furthermore, that "religion" or the "religious" is intimately tied with experience, while "knowledge" is both distinct from the "religious," yet in some indeterminate relation with it. The juxtapositive "and" does not clarify whether the relation between the two is antagonistic, harmonious, linear, co-determining, even antagonistic. The little clarity the title affords seems to suggest at least two hypotheses: a distinction between knowledge and experience, and that the religious, whatever else it may be, pertains more directly to experience than to knowledge.

These musings on the chapter's heading are an analogue of the discussions between Iqbal and Nazir Niazi, the only translator of *The Reconstruction* whose work was conceived during Iqbal's lifetime.[14] Niazi's project sprang out of numerous conversations and letters between the two. In his preface to his translation, Niazi comments that he himself initiated the project of an Urdu translation, to which the author agreed. Niazi did not imagine or desire to do the work himself, but the responsibility eventually fell on his shoulders, after Iqbal granted him permission. But Iqbal had first required Niazi to visit him in Lahore and produce "sample" translations, especially of the second chapter. Iqbal discussed the drafts with Niazi, corrected them, and standardized translations of the book's more technical conceptual language.[15]

Iqbal, who is one of the most significant Urdu and Persian poets of the twentieth century, suggested that Niazi translate the first chapter's title, "Knowledge and Religious Experience" as "*ʿilm bi-al-ḥavās aur ʿilm bi-al-vaḥī*" – knowledge through the senses (*ḥavās*) and knowledge through revelation (*vaḥī*).[16] Iqbal's recommendation of *ʿilm bi-al-vaḥī* (knowledge through revelation) suggests that "religion" or the "religious" in *The Reconstruction* is not confined to "experience" or the "experiential" but also in some way includes "knowledge." His recommendation of *ʿilm bi-al-ḥavās* (knowledge through the senses) suggests that knowledge is related to some sort of source (senses, revelation) "through" which it emerges and to which it is linked. Iqbal's recommended translation for "Knowledge and Religious Experience" offers a glimpse of how *The Reconstruction* tries to articulate and relate the concepts of knowledge, experience, and reality. In the paragraphs below, I gather features the volume attributes to these concepts and clarify how the three are related to each other.

The Reconstruction attributes various features to knowledge. Knowledge consists in "the establishment of connexions with the reality that confronts [the claimant]."[17] It is a name for the various processes whereby an inquirer negotiates their environment.[18] There are various "domains of human knowledge."[19] Knowledge is "sense perception elaborated by understanding,"[20] but we cannot "assume, without criticism, that our knowledge of the external world through sense-perception is the type of all knowledge."[21] "In all knowledge there is an element of passion,"[22] yet, in any given sphere of knowledge production, an inquirer actively and critically attempts to "eliminate all subjective elements."[23] Human knowledge "always means discursive knowledge,"[24] and "the character of man's knowledge is conceptual,"[25] but there are contexts where "thought is reduced to a minimum."[26] Knowledge is a means of picturing and "capturing"[27] things as well as to "predict and control" them.[28] Knowledge may be conceptual, non-conceptual, a way to picture or capture reality or an instrument to master and manipulate it.[29] Broadly considered, knowledge is a name for various and contradictory forms of relation that may obtain between an agent of knowledge and that which is known.[30]

In order to signal the environment of a potential knowledge claim, Iqbal employs the concept of "experience." There are different "aspects of human experience,"[31] "regions of human experience,"[32] various "levels of human experience,"[33] numerous "vista[s] of experience."[34] The term "experience" also gestures towards the mediated character of knowledge. Experiences from all sorts of contexts, vistas, regions, and levels can yield "knowledge by interpretation."[35] "For the purposes of knowledge,"[36] experiences are interpreted from variegated environments. The "data of experience" are the "subject" of different enterprises of knowing.[37] To know something (or someone) is to be related with it by means of some form of experience. Experience is "immediate" and is what is interpreted in order to form relationships with reality.[38]

The term "reality" appears in *The Reconstruction* as the designation of what knowledge and experience refer to. Knowledge and experience are ways of "establishing connexions with the reality that confronts us."[39] Reality invades,[40] confronts,[41] and operates on[42] inquirers in multifarious ways and is interpretable through different registers: "The total-Reality, which enters our awareness and appears on interpretation as an empirical fact, has other ways of invading our consciousness and offers further opportunities of interpretation."[43] In specific disciplines of inquiry, knowledge and experience refer to "certain specific aspects of Reality only and exclude others."[44]

If both knowledge and experience name ways through which people form relationships with reality, how are they distinguishable? Experience, Iqbal tells us, supplies data, which, upon interpretation, generate knowledge of reality. "All experience is immediate"[45] and "yield[s] knowledge by interpretation."[46] But if experience is what relates an experiencer with reality, claiming that it is immediate would seem to suggest that human beings have some sort of unmediated access to reality. This is a claim that – as we saw in the previous paragraphs – the plain sense of *The Reconstruction* contests on several occasions. Overall, *The Reconstruction* seems to be making the following set of claims about the relationship between knowledge, experience, and reality:

- Knowledge (K) is a concept that names a relationship, whose relata are knower and reality.
- The relationship knowledge, with reality, becomes possible for a knower through processes and methods of interpretation.
- Experience (E) names that which is interpreted in order to institute the relationship of knowledge between a knower and reality.
- Experience, then, is a relational concept, whose relata are knower and reality.
- Both knowledge and experience are relational concepts, whose relata are knower and reality. But compared with knowledge, experience is something "immediate."

How can *The Reconstruction* claim that knowledge and experience are *distinct* relational categories while claiming that the relata of these categories are *identical* (knower and reality)? It also seems to state that experience supplies data that "yield knowledge" *through* interpretation and also that experience is an *immediate* disclosure of reality as such. My attempts above to spell out the distinctions between knowledge, experience, and reality in *The Reconstruction* suggest that the text's claims about the relationship between these concepts are somewhat confused. In order to resolve these confusions, we could clarify Iqbal's articulation of knowledge, experience, and reality in the form of three two-part relations between:

- experience and reality, viz., experience as a direct, unmediated disclosure of reality
- knowledge and experience, viz., knowledge as an interpretive and mediated relation with experience
- knowledge and reality, viz., knowledge as a doubly removed relation with reality, with reality related directly with experience, and indirectly with knowledge, which is an interpretation of experience.

We might appear to have achieved a resolution, by reading Iqbal's confusing claims about knowledge, experience, and reality as three two-part relations, but there are two glaring problems here. First, our resolution ends up creating the sort of sharp distinction between knowledge and experience that Iqbal's proposed Urdu translation of "Knowledge and Religious Experience" looks to avoid. Second, our resolution also posits experience as a "window," through which the experiencer can peek at reality as it is, which runs counter to *The Reconstruction*'s claim that experience "supplies data" that acquire meaning and reference only through interpretation and not before it. Our current way of relating knowledge, experience, and reality in *The Reconstruction* is linear. The movement from reality to experience to knowledge is rendered a layered removal, with experience being "direct," unlike knowledge, which names an interpretive relation that starts with experience.

I propose to clarify how the terms knowledge, experience, and reality function in *The Reconstruction* by handling them as three irreducible elements of a relation. Instead of postulating three two-part relations, I suggest that we read (1) experience, (2) what experience and knowledge are about, and (3) how experience and knowledge refer to reality as a display of *The Reconstruction*'s three-part, contextual approach to knowledge. This would make sense of *The Reconstruction*'s claim that both knowledge and experience co-refer to reality in processes of interpretation such that *both* are interpretive ways of engaging with reality and *neither* discloses reality in an unmediated, non-interpretive way.[47]

As I read the categories of knowledge, experience, and reality as a three-part relation, I am going to illuminate and clarify my reading strategy in the light of analytical approaches developed and explicated by semioticians such as Charles Peirce,[48] Charles Morris,[49] Susan Petrelli,[50] Winfried Nöth,[51] and John Deely,[52] among numerous others. Contemporary scholars of religion make productive use of semiotic approaches to clarify a host of complex activities, including ritual performance, pragmatic dimensions of discourse, questions surrounding "transcendence," and comparative analyses of culture.[53] I'm using semiotic vocabulary to clarify my reading strategy because it allows one to handle interpretive relations as a three-part process.[54] The point, as I've stated above, is to make sense of Iqbal's confusing claims about the relationship between knowledge, experience, and reality.

Semioticians advise readers trying to work through a three-part, or "triadic" relation to conceive the elements or participants *not* as *primary* and self-sufficient things, whose interaction generates a *derivative* and composite relationship, but as the kinds of things that exist only *as elements of the relationship* – relata that are "cœval" with the relationship. Semiosis is a paradigm of processes that involve relations whose relata acquire meaning and reference only within those relations. Rather than being already given, "pre-existing entities," the relata (or elements) of semiosis are formal concepts or patterns of relation that constitute the process of semiosis. There are three broad relata or elements involved in this process:

- that which is interpreted (usually named a "sign" or a "sign-vehicle")
- those habits or conditions with respect to which the sign-vehicle is interpreted, including the "conclusions" or results or "determinations" of the interpretive process (the "interpretant")
- that about which an interpretive claim is made (the "object")[55]

How might this vocabulary help us grasp the otherwise confusing three-part relation between knowledge, experience, and reality in *The Reconstruction*? For starters, it would entail handling them all as concepts abstracted from the *interpretive process of knowing*. As concepts or formal rules, the terms "knowledge," "experience," and "reality" would name not "entities," but specific forms or patterns of relation that constitute knowing. None of these concepts would be more "elemental" or "foundational" than the other, since their relationship with each other constitutes the process of knowing. In terms of the basic semiotic distinctions I just drew, experience would name what is interpreted (sign-vehicle), knowledge would name those conditions, processes, and conclusions to which interpretation is carried out (interpretant), and reality would be that about which an interpretive claim is made (object).

All of this is consistent with Iqbal's claims about experience, reality, and knowledge that I sampled above: experience yields knowledge about reality by way of interpretation. In this style of reading, none of the three terms would be more elemental or basic than the other: interpretive knowing does not occur *after* a fully specified experience happens in the face of an *already* specified reality. In this triadic way of reading, each element – knowledge, experience, and reality – becomes specifiable in *the act of knowing or interpreting*.

Wilfred Cantwell Smith's masterful study of "scripture" helpfully illustrates what I mean.[56] Smith conceptualizes (1) a scriptural text, (2) a scripture-reading community, and (3) a scripturally accessible reality as *simultaneous* participants in the process of scriptural interpretation, none of which is more elemental, prior, or basic. Smith notes emphatically that no text is scriptural by itself; no community is scriptural before it receives and interprets a text as scriptural; no transcendent reality is signified by a scriptural text before communal interpretation.[57] I'm suggesting that *The Reconstruction*'s categories of knowledge, experience, and reality function in the same vein: no experience refers to reality by itself, no knowledge is possible without engagement with some "region" of experience, and no reality is signified by an experience prior to its interpretation.

This strategy also helps us make sense of Iqbal's claim that experience is "immediate" and that, simultaneously, "things are not given in immediate experience as . . . already possessing definite contours."[58] The "immediacy" of experience does not, then, mean that experience is "about reality" in a more direct way than knowledge is "about reality." In this style of reading, the immediacy of experience signals its *unspecifiability* in the absence of some process of interpretation rather than its *non-interpretive disclosure* of reality. As an element of the process of knowing, experience would acquire aboutness and referentiality only by becoming "subject to interpretation," and not in any non- or pre-interpretive sense. Knowledge (interpretant), experience (sign-vehicle), and reality (object) all acquire referentiality cœvally. They become meaningful simultaneously, and none is more "basic" than the other.

Thus there is no *already-specified* reality *that precedes* the activity of knowing, and on which knowing "builds" in the form of an edifice or structure. *The Reconstruction* proposes that a knower's environment becomes specifiable and knowable in and through practices of knowing. As you can see, this contrasts with Sir Syed, for whom the object of knowledge is absolved from the activities that specify it. The contrast between the two thinkers' approaches becomes sharper in view of an essay by Iqbal where he reflects on the epistemic consequences of the theory of relativity:

> Is the thing known independent of the act of knowledge? Or, is the act of knowledge a constitutive element in the making of the object? Objective reality as understood by [pre-Einsteinian] Physical Science is entirely independent of the act of knowledge. Knowing does not make any difference to it. It is there whether one knows it or not. In studying its behaviour the act of knowledge can be ignored. Thus, Physics ignored Metaphysics in the sense of a theory of knowledge in its onward march. But this attitude of Physical Science, though highly advantageous to itself, could not have been maintained for a long time. The act of knowledge is a fact among other facts of

> experience . . . Einstein . . . has taught us that the knower is intimately related to the object known, and that the act of knowledge is a constitutive element in the objective reality.[59]

Iqbal is quick to guard against any expansively relativistic interpretations of relativity theory and, in *The Reconstruction*, writes against Wildon Carr's construction of a "Monadistic Idealism" on the back of the theory's philosophical consequences.[60] For Iqbal, the reality with which a knower forms relationships certainly *exceeds the knower*, but this reality becomes namable, specifiable, relatable, and interpretable in and through specific experiences and habits of knowing.

John Deely provides a helpful way of avoiding overly idealistic readings of triadic interpretive approaches to knowledge. Following Jakob von Uexküll and others, Deely distinguishes between the interpretive environment in which an organism has its life and the broader world within which the *interpretive environment* has its life.[61] In these terms, Iqbal's triad of knowledge, experience, and reality means that the knower accesses the broader world through the interpretive environment in which they conduct the act of knowing, and not in any unmediated way.

I've suggested in this section that we read "knowledge," "experience," and "reality" in *The Reconstruction* as irreducible elements of its three-part conception of the process of knowing. This reading strategy allows us to make sense of the volume's claim that both knowledge and experience "co-refer" to reality and that experience is both immediate and non-specific. My proposal helps us make sense of the book's claim that different "regions" and "vistas" of experience, engaged by different processes and methods, refer to different "aspects of reality." In the following section, I explore how Iqbal's three-part conception of knowing affects how *The Reconstruction* conceptualizes religion and its relationship with science.

II

Iqbal's reflections on knowledge, experience, and reality underlie a consistent and overarching refrain that animates *The Reconstruction*. Namely, religion, whatever else it may be, is born out of "concrete experience" and relates its practitioners with reality. The book uses a whole host of terms to elucidate the context whose interpretation generates religion, for example, revelation, religious experience, mystical experience, and *waḥī*. I read Iqbal's remarks about religious experience as indicating a two-pronged formal commitment about religion operative in *The Reconstruction*. First, religion names an epistemically fecund interpretive activity and, second, religion is not an epiphenomenon, beneath which something more basic and elemental is at play.

First: for Iqbal, religion or the religious names an interpretive (or semiotic) activity that involves specifiable forms of experience (sign-vehicles), applies specifiable interpretive methods (interpretants), and enables relationships with reality (objects). He notes that religion or the religious emerges out of a specific or unique form of "knowledge-yielding" experience between a foundational figure – Prophets being the prototype – and reality. These experiences are amply attested to and interpreted in the "revealed and mystic literature of mankind,"[62] and their paradigms are Prophetic claims about revelatory relationships with God.[63] Iqbal observes: "Religion aims at reaching the real significance of a special variety of human experience."[64]

Second: when an inquirer encounters a claim that purports to interpret religious or revelatory experience, such an inquirer should avoid imagining that claim as epiphenomenal vis-à-vis something more elemental, which the inquirer can describe more accurately than the claimant. It will simply not do to assert that a claim to revelation finds meaning and value only with respect to some other domain of reference, such as biology, history, philosophy, politics, or psychology.[65] Such an approach is tantamount to treating the claim as an inferior datum[66] while privileging a biological, historical, or psychological claim as a more accurate description of what the revelatory claim is "actually about." Iqbal notes that "religious beliefs and dogmas . . . are not interpretations of those data of experience which are the subject of the sciences of Nature . . . [Religion] aims at interpreting a totally different region of human experience – religious experience – the data of which cannot be reduced to the data of any other science."[67] Iqbal here is refuting a pernicious consequence of representationalism: imagining that an inquirer's epistemic regime lets them peer "behind" the terms expressing the subject matter of their inquiry and glimpse – unhampered by that matter's obfuscations – at what the subject matter is "really" about.

Iqbal's two-pronged formal commitment – religion is epistemically fecund and is not epiphenomenal – does not necessitate some form of "fideism" for engaging with revelatory claims. Instead, it responds to and corrects a two-pronged conceptual error, which, Iqbal avers, renders inquiries into religion both dangerous and dogmatic: first, that human experience is of a generic character and, second, that a specifiable structure of analysis is appropriate for analyzing any and all possible experience.

The first prong assumes that some uniform features of human experience form the seedbed for all possible knowledge claims. Using religious experience as a flagship case, Iqbal argues that, despite the protestations of some of his contemporaries, one cannot "start with the assumption that all experience other than the normal level of experience is impossible."[68] "The whole religious literature of the world, including the records of specialists' personal experiences . . . is a standing testimony to [religious experience]. These experiences are perfectly natural, like our normal experiences."[69]

Even if we put aside seemingly "unusual" but "perfectly natural" religious experience, Iqbal notes that the experience that different natural sciences interpret is not *identical.* Biologists, physicists, and psychologists interpret different "data" or "regions" of experience, and the conflation of such data constitutes a grave intellectual error. Iqbal notes that any given discipline of inquiry has "a special set of facts to observe,"[70] irreducible to the kinds of phenomena that other disciplines handle. To assume that human experience has certain generic characteristics is to assume that a dimension of human experience discloses certain characteristics of reality as such, independent of the context or method or process of inquiry through which it is engaged. In semiotic terms, the first conceptual error consists in assuming that certain sign-vehicles are related with an object, such that they come equipped with some generically available information about the object, which the interpreting environment either grasps or fails to grasp.

The second prong of the conceptual error is the assumption that a single or some specifiable structures of analysis are appropriate to all possible experience. Iqbal states that to assume that reality "invades" our consciousness in the form of data accessible by a *single* structure of analysis is dogmatic.[71] "The concepts we use in the organization of knowledge are . . . sectional in character, and their application is relative to the level of experience to which they are applied."[72] In semiotic terms, this second error is to assume that a specifiable habit of interpretation or set of methods adequately furnishes a schematic for knowing as such. Hidden beneath this sort of grand claim is the likely over-generalization of categories of analysis that emerge out of a specific practice to all possible knowledge claims. The shape of this error in philosophical writings is exemplified by approaches akin to Kant's. Iqbal, although he praises Kant in *The Reconstruction*, notes that to assume with Kant or analogous to him that the architectonics of all possible knowledge is specifiable in the form of exhaustive or universal categories is to assume that our analysand (say, religion) is subservient to some a priori philosophical framework adequate for all our conceptual needs.[73]

Both these conceptual errors – the assumptions that certain privileged experiences disclose the character of reality as such and that certain conceptual schemes exhaustively interpret experience – warp religion and religious claims into two inadequate shapes. The assumption that certain experiences or conceptual schemes are foundational and disclose the true essence of religion configures religion as either an outmoded way of making claims about the world or an outmoded way of organizing social life. These errors end up treating religion as epistemically barren and derivative of something more basic and elemental.

Iqbal describes epistemic environments that consider religion an obsolete way of talking about the world in the following terms: "Religion [is taken to be] a pure fiction created by . . . mankind with a view to find a kind of fairyland . . . [For such approaches] religious beliefs and dogmas . . . are no more than merely primitive theories of Nature, whereby mankind has tried to redeem Reality from its elemental ugliness and to show it off as something nearer to the heart's desire than the facts of life would warrant."[74] Such an epistemic environment accepts a certain form of human experience as "normal" and "fact" and "rejects its other levels as mystical and emotional."[75] It disqualifies not just the contents of certain knowledge claims, but a priori rejects certain forms of claims as unreasonable.

Typically, in such an environment, human experience is analyzed as composed out of sense data, which are subjected to interpretation, to yield knowledge. Iqbal rejects that, for all contexts of knowing, it is useful to assume that human experience is composed of elemental "sense impressions." This interpretation of the character of human experience may be a useful hypothesis in certain contexts of knowing – Iqbal names physics as such a context – but as a generalization about experience as such, it a priori excludes certain knowledge claims. In fact, Iqbal argues, positing sense impressions as the ground for any and all knowledge claims disqualifies biology and psychology as practices of knowing.[76]

Even some day-to-day, functional certainties disappear if sense impressions are treated as the only way to capture human experience.

For instance, it becomes difficult to sustain the claim that in our "social intercourse" we are in the presence of and commerce with "other minds." We hypothesize that other human beings possess will, thought, desires, and hopes not because we possess some sense organ that can perceive those qualities. Instead, "our fellows are known to be real because they respond to our signals and thus constantly supply the necessary supplement to our own fragmentary meanings."[77] These "signals" or "responses," rather than sense impressions, fund hypotheses about other humans as wilful, thoughtful, desiring, hopeful beings.

Assuming that all possible experience is composed of sense impressions tends to bend religion or religious claims into an inadequate shape – a means of making claims about the external world that provided "primitive" human beings with "theories of Nature." "Religion is not physics or chemistry, seeking an explanation of Nature," Iqbal asserts.[78] If religious claims are treated as analyses of sense data, then they display to a contemporary investigator how human beings in the "past" devised vocabularies, techniques, and methods to explain and understand the world around them. In the present, the modern natural sciences perform the function of describing the world human beings live in and improve on "religious theories" about it, which, in the wake of the sciences, seem to rely on superstitious and fantastic claims about angels, prophets, scripture, miracles, the *jinn*, the day of judgment, eschaton, and so on.

Iqbal describes epistemic environments that take religion to be an antiquated way of organizing social life in the following terms: "The implication of these theories, on the whole, is that religion does not relate the human ego to any objective reality beyond himself; it is merely a kind of well-meaning biological device calculated to build barriers of an ethical nature round human society in order to protect the social fabric . . . according to [such theories], Christianity has already fulfilled its biological mission."[79]

This analysis reduces religious claims to subjectivity, and their import is the generation of different forms of social and political order. Whereas the adherents and practitioners of religion may imagine that religion names, for instance, an encounter between the divine and the human, scientific inquiry discloses that religion is a name for structures of authority, control, and socialization. Religion becomes a form of narrative construction that expresses the subjective or internal desires, hopes, states of consciousness of the constructors of religious narratives. To a contemporary investigator, religion and religious claims display vocabularies, techniques, and methods human beings employed in the past for describing themselves and social reality. This function is performed more adequately in the present by psychology and other human sciences. Iqbal argues that inquiries into the political, psychological, or other dimensions of the context of religion or religious experience are not *substitutive*: "[It is impossible] to undo the spiritual value of the mystic state by specifying the organic conditions which appear to determine it . . . Psychologically speaking, all states, whether their content is religious or non-religious, are organically determined. The scientific form of mind is as much organically determined as the religious."[80]

Both ways of seeing religious claims – either as primitive objectivity or as primitive subjectivity – conceive them as "reports" that express either some external feature of the claimant's environment or some internal feature of the claimant, which some more accurate, more scientific discipline of inquiry such as physics or psychology can better express. In either case – whether religious claims are traceable to the mists of subjectivity or are historically significant but now superseded theories of nature – religion or the religious is an epiphenomenal something, traceable to more elemental things disclosed by some contemporary discipline of inquiry. Religion becomes a way of describing the physical world or a way of expressing and controlling psychological needs or desires. Inquiry into religion, then, becomes about going behind religious claims and "unveiling" the verities religious vocabulary imperfectly expresses.

I'm going to express formally the shape of the errors in conceptualizing religion that disturb Iqbal to provide a handy summary. It will also help us see more clearly, in the next section, how Iqbal re-enacts the epistemological errors he criticizes:

- Some inquirer or context of inquiry (C_1) confronts someone or some other context of inquiry (C_2) that makes certain claims (A_2) about some object (R). Or C_1 reads: C_2 says A_2 about R.
- In C_1 any claim (A) about any object (R) has to obey the standards of knowing operative in C_1. Or: Any A about R should be according to C_1.
- C_2 is not identical to C_1. This is evidence to suppose that A_2 is a misstatement about R and requires revision.
- A_2, clarified and revised according to C_1, becomes claim A_1. Hence, A_2 about R, re-read properly, is actually A_1 about R.
- C_2 clarified and revised, then, would become C_1.

Iqbal is critical of regimes of knowing (C_1) that, as they come across claims (A_2) issued from some other context (C_2), cannot help but assimilate those claims into their own norms, terms, and conventions, thereby re-reading A_2 as A_1. The polemical dimensions of so reshaping inquiries into religion are captured well by Revs. Henry Elliot and Henry Tucker's remarks in 1858 on how nineteenth-century colonial educational institutions shape Indian students:

> He [the student] enters the school premises, becomes acquainted with mathematical science, with astronomy and geometry. Naturally, he loses confidence in his own religion when he finds that it contains so many ridiculous and impossible explanations. Propositions of Euclid and Sir Isaac Newton confute the fables . . . of their religion . . . It is impossible, even if we wished it, to be absolutely neutral in dealing with the false religions of India; for they are so intimately blended with false science that we cannot teach the simplest lessons . . . without contradicting the false sciences contained in their religious books [thereby] proving their religions themselves to be false.[81]

Iqbal intervenes in this polemically charged epistemological environment to propose seeing experience, the "subject-matter of interpretation," as having various "levels" and "regions" that are interpreted by different methods of investigation. Thus he refers to experience at the levels variously of "matter," of "life," and of "consciousness," which form the subject matter of physics, biology, and psychology, respectively.[82]

In fact, the term "experience" rarely appears in *The Reconstruction* without some specification of its "region" or "level."[83] Religious experience is one such "level" or "region" available for human interpretation and exploration: "Religious beliefs and dogmas . . . are not interpretations of those data of experience which are the subject of the sciences of Nature. Religion is not physics or chemistry seeking an explanation of Nature in terms of causation; it really aims at interpreting a totally different region of human experience – religious experience – the data of which cannot be reduced to the data of any other science."[84]

I read these claims by Iqbal as his attempt to articulate some pattern of relation, C_3, that makes peace between claims that emerge in C_1 and C_2. He suggests that any practice of inquiry, C_1, when it comes across claims (A_2) from another context (C_2), *should treat such claims and contexts as forms of inquiry* rather than merely as "subject-matter" that passively awaits C_1 to dissect and display it. One can ease the conflict between religion and science by conceiving the two sets of practices as inquiries with different habits and subject matters of interpretation. Thus religion names those human practices, habits, and institutions that interpret and analyze a specific form of human experience, which Iqbal calls "religious" or "mystical." Similarly, the various sciences name those human practices, institutions, forms of analyses that deal with other forms of experience, at, for instance, "the level of matter [physics], the level of life [biology], and the level of mind and consciousness [psychology]."[85]

The various sciences, too, would be at war like religion and science, if they failed to view each other as distinct contexts of interpretation, handling non-identical subject matters. "Their conflict [i.e., religion and science] is due to the misapprehension that both interpret the same data of experience."[86] Both seek excellence in their enactment. Interpreting human experience, and thereby making potentially trustworthy and dependable claims about reality, are concerns as much of religion as of science.

Prophets, the communities they engage with, and the traditions of practice that emerge in the form of "religious communities" develop methods and techniques of interpreting religious experience. Iqbal's general argument is that prophets, theologians, mystics, and jurists are just as concerned with "objectivity" in their sphere of activity as scientists are in theirs.[87] Inquiries into the meaning of revelation are "genuine effort[s] to clarify human consciousness . . . [and are] as critical of [their] level of experience as Naturalism is of its own level."[88] Religious traditions are constituted by such practices of interpretation, examination, and emulation.

Iqbal gives the illustration of a Sufi practitioner, who "passes from experience to experience, not as a mere spectator, but as a critical sifter of experience who by the rules of a peculiar technique, suited to his sphere of inquiry, endeavours to eliminate all subjective elements, psychological or physiological, in the content of his experience with a view finally to reach what is absolutely objective."[89] Iqbal likens the efforts of a Sufi practitioner to the processes and performances that constitute any given practice of science: "The truth is that the religious and the scientific processes, though involving different methods, are identical in their final aim. Both aim at reaching the most real."[90]

Iqbal's efforts at making peace between religion and science employ a triadic or contextual conception of knowing. He re-describes the two as different forms of interpretive activity. As I said above, *The Reconstruction* seeks to articulate a rule of relation C_3 such that claims from C_2 are not assimilated into the norms, terms, and conventions of C_1. In the next section I show how Iqbal's own practice of conceptualizing religion, rather than performing C_3, generates a practice that transforms religion and the religious into the terms of *his* own discourse.

III

The Reconstruction's conceptualization of religion becomes representational as Iqbal examines mystical experience. After indicating that lack of time prevents a detailed discussion,[91] he attributes five "main characteristics" to mystical experience.

First, mystical experience yields knowledge by interpretation. It, like any other form of human experience, is "immediate" – hence, as we have seen above, "subject to interpretation,"[92] like other "regions" or "levels" of human experience that yield knowledge of reality via interpretive processes: "As regions of normal experience are subject to interpretation . . . for our knowledge of the external world, so the region of mystic experience is subject to interpretation for our knowledge of God."[93]

Second, mystical experience displays "unanalysable wholeness." This is not to suggest something eerie: the "same Reality"[94] that operates on us in ordinary circumstances engages us here too – mystical experience is "perfectly natural." But whereas we normally engage with that same reality in ways that facilitate our everyday practical needs and environment-specific concerns, mystical experience takes us "into contact with the total passage of Reality in which all the diverse stimuli [that operate on us] merge into one another and form a single unanalyzable unity in which the ordinary distinction of subject and object does not exist."[95] Iqbal offers an analogy: we can analyze the ordinary experience of seeing a table placed in front of us as, first, the selection of a finite datum of experience that "fall[s] into a certain order of space and time" out of the "innumerable data of experience" that operate on us, and, second, the synthesis of this selection "into the single experience of the table."[96] Mystical experience is, in contrast, a "single *unanalysable* unity."[97]

Third, mystical experience "is a moment of intimate association with a Unique Other Self [i.e., God], transcending, encompassing, and momentarily suppressing the private personality of the subject of experience."[98]

Fourth, its interpretive fruits are not identical with its actuality. Undergoing a mystical experience is not the same as talking about it: "The interpretation which the mystic or the prophet puts on the content of his religious consciousness can be conveyed to others in the form of propositions, but the content itself cannot be so transmitted."[99] Iqbal explicitly gestures towards "the old theological controversy about verbal revelation"[100] – about how the words that constitute revelation relate to their genesis: whether the words of the Qur'an are themselves revealed or are Muhammad's, whether God speaks Arabic or imprints revelation on the heart of its recipient, who then articulates it.[101] Iqbal rejects distinctions between revelatory experience and its fruits. Its unanalyzable wholeness renders unhelpful arguments over whether it is constituted by "feelings," "ideas," or "words." "There is a sense in which the word is also revealed," says Iqbal.[102]

Fifth, mystical experience is fleeting: it does not permanently dissociate the experiencer from ordinary life; the mystical state "fades away," and allows the person to return to the everyday.[103]

The Reconstruction does not explain how Iqbal reached this understanding of mystical experience, religious experience, or *waḥī*. Scholars have noted that the features Iqbal attributes to mystic experience bear the marks of engagement with and borrowings from various sources: Iqbal's reading of William James and James Ward;[104] his reflections on Rumi and Ḥallāj;[105] his involvement in the *qādiriyyah* Sufi order;[106] and his claims that the words of his poetry are given to him under the spell of inspiration, akin to mystical experience.[107] All these sources offer illuminating material for piecing together how *The Reconstruction* distills the qualities of mystical experience.

As I discuss the representational qualities of Iqbal's reflections on mystical experience, I do not concentrate on its elusive sources, even though, as Nicholas Adams suggests, their opacity renders his discussions in *The Reconstruction* rather assertorial.[108] Where Iqbal makes a claim about, let us say, mystical experience, without indicating its sources, he makes his claims non-contextual and especially hospitable to over-general and binary readings.

I concentrate instead on a more precise marker of Iqbal's representational voice: Iqbal uses the terms mystic experience, religious experience, or *waḥī* as a general concept that defines the "core" of religion. This move implies that concepts derived from Islamic intellectual history that may be adequate for studying Islam's scriptural resources are applicable to the study of any given religious tradition.

As we saw in the previous section, *The Reconstruction* is furiously critical of any conceptual schemes (C_1) that study religion by translating and refashioning religious claims into a priori "moulds." The scholarship Iqbal is writing against traces religion back to more elemental psychological, political, or even physical claims. Iqbal's depiction of mystical experience seems to suggest that *its features* are the terms in which religious claims – emerging from any given environment – should be re-expressed. The way *The Reconstruction* handles the concept of mystical experience does not prevent its performing the kind of substitutive function that Iqbal imagines Freudian and Jungian inquiries into religion perform, as they re-express the traditions of practice they encounter in their own pre-determined conceptual vocabularies. For example, Iqbal notes that religious experience involves a moment of intimate association with God. This particular scheme (C_1), employed for examining religious traditions that do not feature God, would reductively "bend" religious claims from those traditions in the kinds of awkward shapes of which, as we saw above, Iqbal is quite critical and wary.

Iqbal's representational approach emerges again when he divides religious life into three periods: "faith," "thought," and "discovery." Religion begins with "perfect submission" to certain rules and laws, is followed by a "rational understanding of the discipline and the ultimate source of its authority," and culminates in mysticism, where a religious individual discovers "the ultimate source of the law within the depths of his own consciousness."[109] Iqbal offers a conceptual framework – quite akin to the a priori schemes he criticizes elsewhere in *The Reconstruction* – for understanding the history of any religion as a developmental or evolutionary process through successively "law," "metaphysics," and "mysticism." He generalizes categories from the Islamic intellectual tradition, organizes them in a developmental mould, and proposes pouring into it the history of any religious tradition.

Some of Iqbal's reflections on the relationship between religion and science bear the marks of representational approaches he criticizes. We saw in the first section that Iqbal rejects the notion that human beings have some sort of unmediated access to reality. Our claims about reality are mediated by different "regions" of experience. Religion, in this key, interprets "religious experience," just as physics interprets "experience at the level of matter." Yet there are instances in *The Reconstruction* where Iqbal declares that religion offers a more direct and foundational access to reality than other enterprises of knowing: "Science does not care whether its electron is a real entity or not. It may be a mere symbol, a mere convention. Religion, which is essentially a mode of actual living, is the only serious way of handling Reality."[110] And, elsewhere: "Nature as a subject of science is a highly artificial affair . . . Religion [in contrast] demands the whole of reality."[111] Religion offers the possibility of "direct contact"[112] with reality, whereas science explores reality only "indirectly."[113]

While Iqbal's contemporaries argue that religious claims are epistemically empty or epiphenomenal, he articulates a three-part conception of knowing and names religion as *one* avenue or context of inquiry. He then violates this rule and does what he accuses his contemporaries of. If they claim that scientific investigation is privileged vis-à-vis other modes of knowing, he claims that religious contexts have a privileged access to reality and scientific ones are "artificial" and "partial" in comparison.

A far more pronounced instance of Iqbal's representational approach to religion occurs in one of the "base-texts" for *The Reconstruction.*[114] In his "Islam as a Moral and Political Ideal,"[115] Iqbal notes that the task of a "student of religion" is to determine the central "propositions" on which the structure of the entire religion depends.[116] For Iqbal, the central proposition that undergirds Buddhism is that "there is pain in nature."[117] For Christianity, "there is sin in nature,"[118] and for Zoroastrianism "there is struggle in nature."[119] Iqbal then asks: "What is the central ideal in Islam which determines the structure of the entire system?"[120] And he answers: "The central proposition which regulates the structure of Islam … is that there is fear in nature, and the object of Islam is to free man from fear."[121] Islam's ultimate purpose is "freeing humanity from superstition,"[122] from false sources of fear.

Notice that Iqbal's claims about these religions are two-part, over-general formulations that omit the processes and methods whence they emerge. More important, however, as in Sir Syed's approach in chapter 1 above, Iqbal here seeks an elemental something on which the object of his study – Islam, Christianity, Zoroastrianism, and religion more generally – rests. "There is fear in nature, and the object of Islam is to free man from fear," is offered by Iqbal as a foundational claim, on which the "structure of Islam" rests. As in Sir Syed's approach, Iqbal's foundational formula pits him in a competition governed by the law of excluded middle against other inquirers, whose claims about Islam's central proposition are identical to or in competition with Iqbal's.

The Reconstruction enacts this kind of competition by claiming that Islam's "original core" has historically become overlain with a "Magian crust" and Iqbal seeks a vision of "Islam as emancipated from its Magian overlayings."[123] His task then is to recover Islam's original, anti-Magian spirit, veiled over the ages by Greek philosophy, Arab imperialism, and Persian mysticism.[124] His recovery of Islam's core pits it in binary competition against other such visions.

In fact, religions in general are in competition with each other, based, as they are, on different central propositions about the world. Is there, finally, pain in nature? Or sin, or fear? Just as Iqbal's identification of Islam's core is for him truer than rival articulations, Islam itself becomes the ideal form of religion, in competition with other religions. For instance, he sees Islam, by virtue of the propositions that structure it, as best able to relate to modern science. Christianity is not quite so fortunate.[125] Iqbal claims that Islam's "standpoint" is melioristic. And meliorism is "the ultimate presupposition and justification of all human effort at scientific discovery and social progress."[126] Islam's central values, which *The Reconstruction* identifies as freedom, equality, and solidarity, are also amenable to the modern age in ways that other religious traditions and their values may not be. Iqbal notes that in Islam the "essence of *Tawhid* [the oneness of God], as a working idea, is equality, solidarity, and freedom,"[127] but:

> The pure brow of the principle of *Tawhid* has received more or less an impress of heathenism, and the universal and impersonal character of the ethical ideals of Islam has been lost through a process of localization. The only alternative open to us, then, is to tear off from Islam the hard crust which has immobilized an essentially dynamic outlook on life, and to rediscover the original verities of freedom, equality, and solidarity with a view to rebuild our moral, social, and political ideals out of their original simplicity and universality.[128]

Iqbal's approach displaces the competition between science and religion and reintroduces it between various religious traditions by reading them as structures built on foundational assumptions. The house of Islam is securer than the houses of other religions because its basic principles are truer. This way of conceiving religious traditions almost assumes the polemical tenor of approaches towards the study of religion that Iqbal criticizes. In a newspaper article where Iqbal thematizes the relationship between Islam and nationalism, he writes: "The history of religions conclusively shows that in ancient times religion was national as in the case of Egyptians, Greeks and Persians. Later on, it became racial as that of the Jews. Christianity taught that religion is an individual and private affair . . . It was Islam and Islam alone which, for the first time, gave the message to mankind that religion was neither national and racial, nor individual and private, but purely human and that its purpose was to unite and organise mankind despite all its natural distinctions."[129]

Iqbal's over-general conceptual vocabulary for handling mystical experience, combined with his reading of religions as systems, each grounded on a basic proposition, leads him to hermeneutical war on multiple fronts: between his identification of the "core" of religion and other accounts that may posit rival "kernels" of religion; between his identification of each religion's basic proposition and rivals' arguments; and, finally, between various "religious systems," each standing on its own "basic facts." On each front, Iqbal's representational voice commits him to descriptive, foundational, binary, and essentialist claims. *Waḥī* emerges as the proper way to talk about religion; freedom, equality, and liberty emerge as Islam's "basic values"; the history of Islam becomes the history of a Persian and Magian crust forming over an original Arab core; and Islam emerges as a victorious combatant, in its war against more "national," more "individuated," less adequate "religious systems."

Before I move on to another set of themes in the next chapter, I would like to give my readers an outline of the interplay between Iqbal's representational and pragmatic voices in relation to the themes of this chapter. My purpose is, first, to offer a clear picture of the epistemological practices Iqbal criticizes, corrects, and repeats vis-à-vis knowledge, experience, and reality and, second, to show how these concepts affect his conception of religion, science, and their interrelation.

Iqbal *criticizes* epistemological approaches that imagine religion is an epiphenomenon and that religious claims are primarily descriptions, either of the physical world or of the needs and desires of religious subjects. Such approaches conceive religion as a set of descriptive reports and presuppose that other disciplines of knowing such as physics and psychology carry out the primary function of religious claims (describing the world or describing human desires and needs) more accurately. Physics and psychology can look "behind" religious claims and uncover their "essence," which religious claims describe in imperfect ways. Iqbal traces these approaches to religion to two epistemic assumptions: that either a set of conceptual schemes (e.g., psychology, physics) or a set of experiences (e.g., sense experience) form a privileged, foundational mould for shaping any subject matter of analysis.

Iqbal *corrects* such approaches with a three-part, contextual conception of knowledge, wherein experience does not have a generically specifiable character but acquires its features in the process of interpretation. Conceptual schemes, similarly, are relative to their context or subject matter of analysis. Knowledge claims are not foundationally justified descriptions but interpretive ways of forming various relationships with reality. Religion names those human practices, habits, institutions, and forms of analyses covering a specific form of human experience, which Iqbal calls "religious" or "mystical." Similarly, the various sciences name those human practices, institutions, and forms of analyses that relate to other, non-identical dimensions of human experience.

Iqbal *repeats* the epistemological errors he criticizes when he proposes variously that the concept of mystical experience or revelation is well-suited for understanding any religious tradition; that every religion rests on a "central proposition," which an inquirer seeks to describe; that Iqbal's task is to uncover Islam's "essence," beneath its Magian crust; and that religious experience gives better, more "direct contact" with reality than other explorations of human experience.

Iqbal most effectively repairs representational tendencies when he applies a three-part contextual framework to correct foundationalist and essentialist conceptions of knowledge. He corrects frameworks that take certain experiences or conceptual schemes to be epistemically privileged and exhaustive by arguing that we ought to see experiences and conceptual schemes as having various "levels" and "regions." His repair falters, for instance, in his articulation of the shape of revelatory experience or in his exhaustive and privileged explanation of the core of Islam. His "advice" on how to relate knowledge, experience, and reality is reparative, but his own work on revelatory experience or the history of Islam repeats the mistakes he attacks. In the next chapter, we see that Iqbal pragmatically corrects descriptive, foundationalist, and essentialist ways of thinking about physics and biology but ignores his own corrections in relation to psychology.

CHAPTER THREE

The Cosmos as Self

The previous chapter explained how the concepts of knowledge, experience, and reality function in Muhammad Iqbal's *The Reconstruction*. I showed that Iqbal uses them to argue that the norms and conditions that render knowledge valid and reliable are not reducible to the norms of a finite and specifiable discourse such as biology, history, or physics. He claims that religion names those human practices, habits, and institutions that find their legitimation in *waḥī*, religious experience, or mystical experience. He offered his claims to an intellectual habitus that sought to peer behind religious claims in order to extract what they are truly about. I concluded by showing how Iqbal's own practice of conceptualizing mystical experience as the core of religion re-performs problematic practices of reasoning he criticizes in *The Reconstruction*.

In this chapter I conduct an analogous, two-part exercise with *The Reconstruction*'s use of the concept of *khudi* (selfhood). First, I discuss the concept's functions in the book and how it helps Iqbal conceive of religion and its relations with science, pulling together knowledge claims from various disciplines of inquiry. Second, I delve into how Iqbal portrays physics, biology, and psychology as disciplines relating their practitioners with God. I show how, in using the concept of *khudi* to develop this framework, Iqbal offers a unique and unusual "proof of God." His second-order reflections on physics and biology turn out to be pragmatic, whereas he looks at psychology through a representational lens.

I

The concept of *khudi*, which Iqbal renders in English variously as self, selfhood, individuality, personality, and ego, permeates not just *The Reconstruction*, but all of his philosophy and poetry. Two of his most celebrated Persian works are *Asrār-i Kẖūdī* (Secrets of the Self) and *Rumūz-i Bekẖūdī* (Mysteries of Selflessness),[1] while several of his Urdu poems have the term in their titles.[2] In his Urdu preface to the first edition of *Secrets of the Self*, he discusses the scope of his concerns: "This mysterious thing, which binds the dispersed and unbounded facets of human nature,[3] this self, or me, or I, which becomes visible in its activity and remains hidden in reality, which is creative of all observation but whose subtlety cannot bear the warm gaze of observation; what is this thing?"[4] In his English preface to R.A. Nicholson's translation of the work, he depicts individuality as a pervasive category, as an irreducible, "fundamental fact of the universe."[5]

Iqbal has been widely described as the "philosopher of *khudi* (selfhood)."[6] Mustansir Mir,[7] Javed Majeed,[8] Souleymane Bachir Diagne,[9] Mohammad Rafiuddin,[10] J.J. Houben,[11] Alessandro Bausani,[12] Aziz Ahmad,[13] Riffat Hassan,[14] Hafeez Malik,[15] and Richard Wheeler,[16] among numerous others, have discussed the way *khudi* or selfhood functions in Iqbal's thought. Shahab Ahmed, in his expansive study of Islamic concerns with subjectivity and selfhood, succinctly captures the function of *khudi* vis-à-vis religion and modernity in Iqbal's philosophical thought. After arguing that "questions about the meaning and constitution of Self have been central to the discourses of Muslims from very early in history . . . [arising] directly from the Muslim predicament of making meaning by engagement with the phenomenon of Revelation,"[17] Ahmed observes:

> A signal instance of the focus on the Self as locus for the Truth and Meaning of Islam (in some ways the historical culmination of this idea) comes with the (re-)mobilization by the philosopher, poet, and reformer, Muḥammad Iqbāl, of the millennium-old Persian/Urdu concepts of *khwudī*, literally, 'Self-ness,' or 'Self-hood,' and *bī-khwudī*, literally: 'without-Self-ness' or 'Self-less-ness,' as the seminal concepts for the (self-)creation of a new twentieth-century species of Muslim capable of meeting the challenges of modernity.[18]

The Reconstruction employs *khudi* to help construct an interpretive context wherein revelation is a potential source of trustworthy knowledge claims. As Ahmed points out, concepts involving selfhood, such as self-affirmation, self-articulation, self-contemplation, and self-interrogation, are closely linked to the meaning of revelation throughout Islamic intellectual history.[19] Iqbal uniquely offers it to an intellectual context that, he perceives, reduces revelatory or mystical experience to the terms of the natural and human sciences. Modernity, insofar as it deprecates revelatory claims as a matter of principle, poses a threat and a challenge. Doubly so, if modern discourse claims that, in addition to such claims being suspect, *only* its own canons can assess them. As Shahab Ahmed notes, Iqbal uses the concept of *khudi* to create "a new twentieth-century species of Muslim capable of meeting the challenges of modernity."[20]

How does Iqbal render revelation a trustworthy source of knowledge by using the concept of *khudi*? He uses it to elaborate an interpretive framework wherein knowledge claims from disciplines such as biology, history, philosophy, physics, and theology may cohere. It is the broadest concept employed in *The Reconstruction*, not bounded by any indexical restrictions and attributable to any and all phenomena that human beings can potentially relate to.[21] By arguing that each and every phenomenon to which human beings can potentially relate is of the character of a self, *The Reconstruction* proffers a worldview for a Muslim community and context of knowing that constructs and trusts narratives involving Prophets, a speaking God, and texts that are received as containing God's speech and communication to Prophets, while, at the same time, engages with the methods, claims, and fruits of the natural and human sciences.

As I show in the next section, Iqbal offers the concept of *khudi* as an outcome of second-order reflection on different practices of knowing. *Khudi* emerges thence to help connect disciplines of knowing that may otherwise delegitimize each other. Iqbal offers it as a corrective to those who abstract concepts from a particular natural or human science and present them as affording a "systematic view" of reality as such.[22] He shows that such an abstractive practice in modern physics, biology, and psychology generates worldviews – such as atomistic materialism and mechanistic evolution – that exclude revelatory claims as truth-bearing.

Iqbal corrects this practice by devising an interpretive framework that can admit the practices of exegesis, theology, biology, physics, history, and so on as knowledge-yielding. *The Reconstruction* does so by arguing that the knowledge claims of any and all practices of knowing can be conceived as interpretations of the activity of (the self of) God. It invokes the concept of selfhood to retrieve what, according to Shahab Ahmed, was a salient feature of the episteme of the pre-colonial Balkans-to-Bengal Islamic complex: ultimately God is the *ḥaqīqah* (Real-Truth) signified in any given practice of knowing.[23]

Because the institutions that have historically shaped and guided the formation of "Muslim subjects" have been disabled in the context of colonial modernity,[24] Iqbal's 1929 auditors – university students in Aligarh, Hyderabad, and Madras – are socialized in "habits of thought" that are epistemologically and spiritually broken.[25] These students' "purely secular education" configures an intellectual habitus wherein the Muslim community's intellectual resources conflict and compete with the intellectual heritage of the west. In "The Muslim Community – A Sociological Study" Iqbal reflects on the absence of a *paideia* to connect classical Islamic discourses such as exegesis (*tafsīr*) and theology (*kalām*) with western philosophy and science:

> In the modern Muslim youngman we have produced a specimen of character whose intellectual life has absolutely no background of Muslim culture without which, in my opinion, he is only half a Muslim or even less than that provided his purely secular education has left his religious belief unshaken. He has been allowed, I am afraid, to assimilate western habits of thought to an alarming extent ... our young man ... is deplorably ignorant of the life-history of his own community ... Intellectually he is a slave to the west ... [His] undivided devotion to an alien culture is a kind of imperceptible conversion to that culture, a conversion which may involve much more serious consequences than conversion to a new religion ... Having been in close touch with the student-life of to-day for the last ten or twelve years, and teaching a subject closely related to religion ... it has been my painful experience that the Muslim Student, ignorant of the social, ethical and political ideals that have dominated the mind of his community, is spiritually dead.[26]

In *The Reconstruction*, *khudi* aids in the construction of a conceptual framework that can non-antagonistically relate Islamic and western "habits of thought."

Iqbal sets up the stage for creating such a framework in *The Reconstruction* by assuming the standpoint of these very students. He points out that they have every right to interrogate knowledge claims that purport to be revelatory.[27] Specifically, if a mystic or a prophet claims to have encountered God and that encounter has yielded certain judgments, how may someone not a witness assess claims of revelatory experience as yielding knowledge and trustworthy?[28] Even more precisely, what sorts of warrants, justificatory processes, and forms of reasoning can assess the Muslim community's confidence in Muhammad's claims to revelatory experience and the Qur'an as a locus of God's speech to Muhammad?

To this end, the second chapter of *The Reconstruction* illustrates a method – an "intellectual test" – to verify claims that an individual offers as the fruits of revelation (*waḥī*). This test is ambitious and complex, preparing the way for arguments about how God is the ultimate reality signified in any given practice of knowing – the focus of the next section of this chapter.

Iqbal describes his "intellectual test" of claims offered as fruits of religious experience in these terms:

> Now when a judgment which claims to be the interpretation of a certain region of human experience, not accessible to me, is placed before me for my assent, I am entitled to ask, what is the guarantee of its truth? Are we in possession of a test which would reveal its validity? . . . Happily we are in possession of tests which do not differ from those applicable to other forms of knowledge . . . *The intellectual test [means] critical interpretation, without any presuppositions of human experience, generally with a view to discover whether our interpretation leads us ultimately to a reality of the same character as is revealed by religious experience.*[29]

I provide below three somewhat formal ways of interpreting what Iqbal's test looks to accomplish. I label them "epistemological," "ontological," and "cognitive-dissonance" models for understanding how Iqbal sets up the possibility of reposing trust in claims that purport to be revelatory.

According to my epistemological model, Iqbal's intellectual test:

- abstracts knowledge claims about reality from a context of inquiry (X) that *The Reconstruction*'s readers may be sceptical of – for instance, theology, Sufism, and qur'anic interpretation
- abstracts knowledge claims about reality from contexts of inquiry that the readers participate in or deem reliable (Y), such as physics, mathematics, biology, and history
- argues that if it is possible to interpret claims from contexts X and Y such that they make "the same" or identical predicative judgments about the character of reality, then inquirers in context Y have good reason to trust X as a reliable context of inquiry.

In the epistemological model, I imagine that Iqbal asks his readers to observe the knowledge claims that emerge from two different epistemological contexts. If the claims are "the same," then these two regimes, perhaps at odds with each other, have warrant to begin to trust each other. If two epistemological regimes appear to be at odds, but make identical claims about what they study, then this should give participants in those regimes pause to re-evaluate their mutual hostility.

In the ontological model:

- If certain practices of inquiry (K_1) are conducted in relation to an object (O_1) in a specific context of inquiry (X) and those practices are interpretable as predicating a set of qualities (a_1, a_2, a_3 . . .) to (O_1),
- and if certain other practices of inquiry (K_2) are conducted in relation to another object (O_2) in another context (Y) and those practices are interpretable as predicating the same set of qualities (a_1, a_2, a_3 . . .) to (O_2),
- then those who participate in and trust the practices of inquiry in Y have some warrant for trusting the practices of inquiry in X. Since K_1 and K_2 refer certain identical predicates to O_1 and O_2, practitioners of K_1 and K_2 may modify their scepticism of each other and entertain the hypothesis that O_1 and O_2 are related to each other.

In the ontological model, I imagine that Iqbal asks his readers to observe, for example, qur'anic exegetes and theologians' claims about the specific objects or beings they study. And then he invites them to observe the claims of, for example, biologists and physicists about their objects of study. The two groups focus on different objects (linguistic marks on a page and atoms, respectively), but if they appear to be making "the same" predicative claims about what they study, then their respective colleagues may ease their mutual scepticism. If the beings that qur'anic exegetes examine (O_1) and the beings that biologists examine (O_2) can be *talked about in identical terms*, the different beings they study *may be related with each other.*

This process of reasoning, *The Reconstruction* suggests, can counter a crisis-inducing and "spiritually deadening" cognitive tendency (K_3) in the intellectual habitus of Muslim university students in India. That tendency characterizes "western" (K_2) and "Islamic" (K_1) "habits of thought" as contradictory. K_3 characterizes K_2 as reliable, modern, consistent, and rational and ascribes the contradictories of these predicates (unreliable, non-modern, inconsistent, irrational) to K_1. More formally, K_3 is the practice of:

- predicating the character of reliability (R) to the norms, objects, and subject matter (b_1, b_2, b_3 . . .) that constitute a practice K_2,
- asserting that any other practice of knowing is R if its norms, objects, and subject matter are describable as b_1, b_2, b_3. Otherwise that practice of knowing is unreliable.
- concluding that if the norms, objects, and subject matter of K_1 and K_2 are not reducible to the same terms, to claim to belong to both K_1 and K_2 is to be cognitively dissonant.

This is what I call a "cognitive-dissonance" model for interpreting Iqbal's "philosophical test of the revelations of religious experience."[30] As we saw in Iqbal's fiery words above, he believed young Muslims were being socialized through a cognitive norm (K_3) that sundered their intellectual universe, rendering one side (modern western norms of knowing – K_2) reliable and the other (classical and medieval Islamic discourse – K_1) unreliable. The purpose of his test is to remedy this "spiritually deadening" cognitive norm.[31]

I offer these three models (epistemological, ontological, cognitive-dissonance) of interpreting Iqbal's intellectual test to elucidate the scope and grammar of his remedial strategies. The focal points of the conflict these strategies address are claims rooted in classical Islamic discourse and those based in modern discourse. Iqbal's strategies establish an interpretive context for conceiving religious or revelatory contexts, along with other contexts of knowing, as valid and reliable.

Iqbal begins his intellectual test – of whether reality is of the "same character" whether interpreted through "religious experience" or through other forms of experience – with scriptural interpretation. This practice predicates a certain "character" to human experience. Iqbal reads a particular verse of the Qur'an (57:3), which he sees as predicating a certain character to reality. According to the Qur'an, Iqbal states, human experience "within and without" refers to and is "symbolic" of God: "The Qur'an . . . regards [human] experience . . . as symbolic of a reality described by it, as '*the First and the Last, the Visible and the Invisible*.'"[32] Thus Iqbal reads a particular verse, which yields the claim that human experience refers to and symbolizes the reality of God. This serves as a claim about reality (O_1) that is generated through a practice (scriptural interpretation) about which Iqbal's readers may be sceptical.

The next step is to "test" this claim via disciplines of inquiry into human experience that Iqbal's readers trust and then examine whether claims from those disciplines can be interpreted as predicating the same character to the forms of experience they interpret. Iqbal engages with physics, biology, and psychology to propose that one may interpret their examinations of human experience such that these sciences, in their own ways, signify the reality of God. In other words, Iqbal takes Q 57:3 to mean that that which revealed itself in the form of speech to Muhammad also reveals itself, in different ways, to those who explore various facets of human experience. We may "plug" Iqbal's specific claim here into the three ways of reading his intellectual test I offered above to elucidate his process of justifying the reliability of religious (in this case, scriptural) claims. The following summaries are simply less abstract versions of those three models:

- The *epistemological* model: Iqbal abstracts a claim about reality through scriptural interpretation; i.e., human experience symbolizes the reality of God. He next argues that modern disciplines of knowing such as physics and biology can be read such that they make an identical claim about reality.
- The *ontological* model: Reading scriptural texts yields a claim about reality. We may explore other facets of reality and find that doing so yields an identical claim about those other facets of reality. Identical claims about different facets of reality suggests that these facets are related to each other.
- The *cognitive-dissonance* model: If Iqbal can convince his readers to trust claims that emerge from classical Islamic discourse and from modern discourse, he can address a "spiritually deadening" tendency operative in his readers' world (K_3): characterizing Islam and modernity in antagonistic and competing terms.

In the next section, I show how Iqbal argues that one can read human experience at "the level of matter, the level of life, and the level of mind"[33] – the "subject-matter of physics, biology, and psychology," respectively[34] – so that their claims refer to God. I explain that Iqbal's arguments are both representational and pragmatic, and I outline his unique warrants for the reality of God.

II

Before Iqbal begins his analyses of physics, biology, and psychology as environments that refer to God in some sense, he summarily dismisses cosmological, ontological, and teleological arguments for the reality of God.[35] He claims that arguments patterned along such lines are abstract and only "superficially" interpret experience, a shortcoming that Iqbal's philosophical test – which harnesses physical, biological, and psychological analyses of experience – looks to remedy.

The Reconstruction's philosophical reflection on physics enacts a two-pronged strategy. Its first prong reveals how this particular experimental science can seem to necessitate conclusions that preclude the possibility of revelatory claims. The second marshals some canon of criticism from within physics that renders those seemingly necessary conclusions unnecessary over-generalizations of concepts employed by physicists. Iqbal begins by showing that "traditional," Newtonian physics assumes a world of matter composed of elemental features, which interacts with the observer or investigator through media such as perception and cognition. Matter in this view is the source of "sense-data," which a physicist analyzes through mathematical tools in order to decipher the behavioural properties and laws that operate in and permeate matter. Iqbal notes that the hypothesis that "experience at the level of matter" consists of independent, self-subsisting things such as particles, laws, and waves, which are the objective source of the (subjective) sense impressions that comprise ordinary consciousness, has facilitated the development of Newtonian physics.[36]

The assumed "distinction between the thing and its [perceived] qualities"[37] animates the hypothesis that, for example, what enters our eyes as we perceive the colour blue is not something blue out there, but waves that oscillate at a certain measurable frequency and length, which the human species subjectively perceives as the colour blue; or that we subjectively perceive sound as being loud or soft or melodious while it is objectively a mechanical vibration of air particles. "When I say, 'The sky is blue', it can only mean that the sky produces a blue sensation in my mind, and not that the colour blue is a quality found in the sky. As mental states they are impressions, that is to say, they are effects produced in us. The cause of these effects is matter, or material things acting through our sense organs, nerves, and brain on our mind."[38]

Such assumptions have allowed Newtonian physics to advance and grow at a remarkable pace. Philosophers and theologians may complain about the epistemological and ontological consequences of hypotheses that have facilitated its advance. They may say, for instance, that the "bifurcation" of human experience into subjective mentality and objective materiality makes us doubt whether knowledge about the world is possible at all.[39] Or they may say that grounding human experience in some form of "pure materiality" is a reductive way to handle the variety of phenomena that constitute human experience.[40] But such criticisms hold weight only *if* we retire physical concepts from the task of manipulating and controlling experimental phenomena and recruit them instead to construct a "view" or picture of reality as such. Iqbal observes that the practices of the modern sciences warrant no such move. Their concepts and theories are not meant to procure "a single systematic view of Reality."[41] "Natural Science . . . if it is true to its own nature and function, [cannot] set up its theory as a complete view of Reality. The concepts we use in the organization of knowledge are . . . sectional in character, and their application is relative to the level of experience to which they are applied."[42]

Iqbal adds that the "theories of science constitute trustworthy knowledge, because they are verifiable and enable us to predict and control the events of Nature."[43] So the philosopher and theologian need not be wary if physicists employ the concepts of material atoms or mechanical causality. Such concepts are valid and reliable to the degree that they allow physicists to precisely examine, control, and predict a certain class of phenomena. Besides, concepts in physics that postulate "a pure materiality" as the subject matter of physics are becoming "unworkable"[44] in the kinds of questions that now occupy physicists. *The Reconstruction* names Einstein and Heisenberg as the chief instigators of novel "domestic difficulties" in the discipline's conceptual apparatuses. The bifurcation of human experience into mentality and materiality, with the latter set aside for physics, may have troubled only philosophers and theologians in the past, but did not affect the conduct of physics. Einstein and Heisenberg transformed that situation: "The scientific view of Nature as pure materiality is associated with the Newtonian view of space as an absolute void in which things are situated. This attitude of science has, no doubt, ensured its speedy progress; but the bifurcation of a total experience into two opposite domains of mind and matter has today forced it [i.e., physics], in view of its own domestic difficulties, to consider the problems which, in the beginning of its career, it completely ignored."[45]

As Iqbal was preparing *The Reconstruction* in the late 1920s, relativity theory and Heisenberg's indeterminacy principle were displaying phenomena seemingly inexplicable if physicists conceived the object of knowledge as independent materiality and the subject of knowledge as reflective mentality. "Einstein . . . has taught us that the knower is intimately related to the object known, and that the act of knowledge is a constitutive element in the objective reality."[46] Physicists were beginning to conceptualize the very concepts of space and time as relative to the frames of reference in which they carried out physical measurements: "The criticism of the foundations of the mathematical sciences has fully disclosed that the hypothesis of a pure materiality, an enduring stuff situated in an absolute space, is unworkable."[47]

Iqbal relies on Bertrand Russell and Alfred North Whitehead's reception of relativity theory to argue for conceptualizing the subject matter of post-Newtonian physics or the specific experience physics interprets "not as a persistent thing with varying states, but a system of inter-related events."[48] This is the key referential claim Iqbal abstracts from his analysis of 1920s' physics. That about which physics makes claims is a system of events or a set of activities in which the observer participates as they attempt to predict and control the things they observe. Physics conceives and interprets its "level of experience" to be a set of inter-related events and activities, rather than substantial somethings that are located in the void of space and persist in time.

Notice the two prongs of Iqbal's argument here. First, if theologians and philosophers find the division of human experience into subjective mentality and objective materiality to be reductive as well as epistemologically and ontologically problematic, they should remind themselves that this bifurcation's primary task is to manipulate and control experimental phenomena, not to provide "a systematic" view of reality. Second, contemporary physicists, because of "domestic debates," have devised concepts that are likely to seem less philosophically and theologically problematic and reductive. The basic claim Iqbal takes away from these debates is that physics conceives of the particular level or kind of experience it analyzes as "inter-related events."

After abstracting this claim, *The Reconstruction* moves on to analyzing experience "at the level of life," the subject matter of biology. Its philosophical reflections on biology enact a different two-pronged strategy. First, *The Reconstruction* shows that biology has used concepts from physics in ways that reduce the subject matter of biological analysis to an epiphenomenon. Second, it discusses the kinds of concepts that contemporary philosophers who engage with biology judge to be appropriate to the field. Iqbal first observes that biology, since

Darwin, has seemed to configure life – the subject matter of its analysis – as an "epiphenomenon," undergirded by mechanistic processes. "All problems, it was believed, were really the problems of physics."[49] This entailed denying that "life" constituted an "independent activity" that required appropriate "concepts of a different order of thought."[50]

It was assumed, Iqbal reports, that biology could simply adopt concepts such as causality and mechanism from Newtonian mechanics and apply them to biological phenomena: "The discoveries of Newton in the sphere of matter and those of Darwin in the sphere of Natural History [seemed to] reveal a mechanism. All problems, it was believed, were really the problems of physics. Energy and atoms, with the properties self-existing in them, could explain everything including life . . . The concept of mechanism – a purely physical concept – claimed to be the all-embracing explanation of Nature."[51]

According to *The Reconstruction*, this mechanistic approach is beginning to change in the early twentieth century. Since "living organisms" behave differently from an "externally worked machine," contemporary biologists and physiologists use concepts such as "purpose" and "ends" to study the "action of living organisms, [which are] initiated and planned in view of an end."[52] Certainly concepts from physics may have some use in examining life, but in the wake of discoveries about the development and growth of biological organisms, these concepts have circumscribed value in biology:

> No doubt, there are aspects of the activity of a living organism which it shares with [non-organic phenomena]. In the observation of these aspects the concepts of physics and chemistry would be needed; but the behaviour of the organism is essentially a matter of inheritance and incapable of sufficient explanation in terms of molecular physics . . . In all the purposive processes of growth and adaptation to its environment, whether this adaptation is secured by the formation of fresh or the modification of old habits, [a living organism] possesses a career which is unthinkable in the case of a machine.[53]

Iqbal relies on J.S. Haldane, Hans Driesch, and Wildon Carr's philosophical reflections on biology to argue that life is explicable in other than mechanistically causal terms. To assume that life is a consequence of certain mathematically describable laws seems to mystify rather than explicate the purposive, goal-driven, and internally regulated behaviour of living organisms. Just as post-Newtonian physicists' expectations of matter are confounded if matter is conceived as self-subsisting materiality, so biologists' expectations vis-à-vis living organisms' behaviour are confounded if they are conceptualized exclusively in mechanical terms. Because the behaviour of living organisms does not reduce to mechanical patterns, and relying on Haldane, Driesch, and Carr, Iqbal ventures: "It would . . . seem that life is foundational and anterior to the routine of physical and chemical processes which must be regarded as a kind of fixed behaviour formed during a long course of evolution."[54]

Iqbal means to suggest not that single-cell organisms "precede" the emergence of helium and oxygen in the universe – only that whatever precedes the emergence and evolution of both physical and biological phenomena cannot be "adequately comprehended" in mechanistic terms alone. Physical concepts are not enough to explain that out of which both simplicity and diversity, mechanism and organism, emerge and evolve. In fact, Iqbal's discussions here refer to early-twentieth-century debates within biology and chemistry between "mechanists," "vitalists," and "emergentists." Figures as wide-ranging as Henri Bergson, Samuel Alexander, Hans Driesch, and Wildon Carr were brought to bear on questions like: What sets biological phenomena apart from physical phenomena? In what ways are physical and biological entities similar? To what degree can mechanical procedures comprehend and explain evolutionary phenomena? Is there some sort of "vital" force that sets apart biological things from physical things?[55]

As Iqbal mentions these conversations, he eschews two positions. First, he challenges the strict mechanists who assimilate and treat the work of biologists as simply an extension of physics.[56] Iqbal sides with the assertion that biology is not simply physics applied to living beings. "The behaviour of [an] organism is essentially a matter of inheritance and incapable of sufficient explanation in terms of molecular physics."[57] Second, Iqbal rejects the idea of a "vital" force that inhabits biological entities and makes them "alive." Life emerges organically out of antecedent phenomena and not by the "insertion" of a mysterious life-force: "There [is no] such . . . thing as a purely physical level in the sense of possessing a materiality, elementally incapable of evolving . . . life and mind."[58] Whatever causes the "sentient and the mental" is "immanent" in the environment where living beings evolve and thrive.[59] Iqbal sides with "emergentist" biological positions that conceive life as purposive, goal-oriented activity and behaviour. This is the key referential claim he abstracts from his analysis of biology. Biology makes claims about purposive, goal-driven activity, which is neither spurred by some mysterious, inscrutable force nor a mere epiphenomenon grounded in some more elemental mechanical activity.

After abstracting this claim, *The Reconstruction* moves on to analyzing experience "at the level of mind," the subject matter of psychology. Its discussion here differs markedly from the way it considers physics and biology as contexts of inquiring into human experience. It here enters a realm of investigation that it takes to be "privileged" vis-à-vis physics and biology.[60] Iqbal's reading of physics and biology emphasizes that their governing concepts are "sectional." They do not afford any "systematic view of reality" or grant unmediated access to reality. As disciplined interpretive enterprises dealing with specific forms of experience, they make claims with respect to some context.

In its analysis of psychology, *The Reconstruction* abandons its contextual employment of the concept of experience.[61] Iqbal argues that the examination of human experience at the level of consciousness discloses something elemental, primal, and non-interpretive that the other sciences do not afford. In contrast to physics and biology, psychology allows us to be in "a position to study [a] privileged case of existence which is absolutely unquestionable."[62] "Now my perception of things that confront me is superficial and external; but my perception of my own self is internal, intimate, and profound. It follows, therefore, that *conscious experience is that privileged case of existence in which we are in absolute contact with Reality*, and an analysis of this privileged case is likely to throw a flood of light on the ultimate meaning of existence."[63]

Psychological analysis, since its subject matter is consciousness itself, affords "absolute contact" with reality, unlocking in the process the "ultimate nature of existence."[64] When we fix our gaze on our own conscious experience, we discover that it is a "perpetual flow," a state of "flux." In "moments of profound meditation,"[65] we may be able to discover that the constant movement and flux of our conscious experience are not arbitrary, capricious, and sense-less. Our conscious experience is organically connected with our past and purposive and goal-directed with respect to the future.[66] The passage of time or duration in our conscious experience is permeated by flux and purpose. Meditation on or focused observation of the purposeful dynamism that permeates it impresses an idea upon the introspective self. Not only am *I* a goal-driven, dynamic centre of life and consciousness, but reality *itself* is of the character of a self. "A critical interpretation of the sequence of time as revealed in our selves" intimates that reality itself is ultimately an organically unified self, in which "thought, life, and purpose interpenetrate."[67]

For *The Reconstruction* this is no ordinary idea. It is an intuitive insight, a "direct revelation of the ultimate nature of Reality."[68] It is this intuitionally grounded, direct vision of reality that Iqbal abstracts from his analysis of experience at the level of consciousness. "Intuition [secured through psychological introspection] reveals life as a centralizing ego."[69] As you can see, Iqbal's reflections on psychology are remarkably different from the way he analyzes physics and biology. Psychological introspection yields an incorrigible insight into the nature of reality as such.

In summary, Iqbal's examination of physics, biology, and psychology yields three abstractions of how these sciences conceive the objects of their examination:

- Experience at the level of matter (physics) yields the claim that reality is a set of inter-related events and activities.
- Experience at the level of life (biology) yields the claim that reality is purposive, goal-driven activity.
- Experience at the level of mind (psychology) yields the claim that reality is a self.

Combining these claims produces the following judgment: reality comprises inter-related events and teleological activity, conducted by a self, an "all-embracing concrete self," or God. Iqbal's intellectual test yields the following judgment: "A comprehensive philosophical criticism of all the facts of experience . . . brings us to the conclusion that the Ultimate Reality is a rationally directed creative life . . . The facts of experience justify the inference that the ultimate nature of Reality is spiritual, and must be conceived as an ego."[70] Thus, Iqbal argues, human experience at the levels of matter, life, and mind refers ultimately to God or the Ultimate Ego, Ultimate Reality, Ultimate Self, Absolute Ego.

Recall that all of Iqbal's intellectual labour aims for a "philosophical test" to prove that non-religious forms of experience reveal the same reality as religious experience. Iqbal undertook his "critical interpretation" of human experience "to discover whether [it] leads us ultimately to a reality of the same character as is revealed by religious experience."[71] His reading of Q 57:3 yielded the claim that "the Qur'an . . . regards [human] experience . . . as symbolic of a reality described by it, as '*the*

First and the Last, the Visible and the Invisible.'"[72] *The Reconstruction* avers that its examination of the subject matter of physics, biology, and psychology warrants the claim that reality is a "rationally directed creative life" – one that revealed itself to Muhammad in the form of speech and does so to the various sciences in different ways.

This intellectual test reinforces *The Reconstruction*'s case for how religion or the religious, whatever else it may be, is a form of inquiry. It also introduces Iqbal's complementary case about science: whatever else it is, science is a form of intimacy with God. Religion is investigative, just as science is worshipful. The practices, institutions, and habits that form both can belong to the same habitus: "The view that we have taken gives a fresh spiritual meaning to . . . science. The knowledge of Nature is the knowledge of God's behaviour. In our observation of Nature we are virtually seeking a kind of intimacy with the Absolute Ego; and this is only another form of worship."[73]

The reception of Iqbal's reading of physics, biology, and psychology as ultimately "God referring" as well as of his theological work more generally in *The Reconstruction* explores several directions. Scholars have investigated the possible intellectual genealogies of Iqbal's theological work, debated and analyzed the "quality" of his argumentation, and explored its constructive and inspirational possibilities.[74] M.M. Sharif – who studied at Cambridge, shared "common teachers"[75] with Iqbal, and attended his "Reconstruction" lecture series at Aligarh in 1929[76] – writes that Iqbal's mature theological reflections, exemplified in *The Reconstruction*, bear the marks of engagements with "Rumi, McTaggart, James Ward, Bergson, and Nietzsche"[77] – especially Ward.[78] For Javed Majeed, Iqbal's writings on theology struggle to articulate a notion wherein "God is both independent of and includes all other selves."[79] One productive route, he suggests, for making sense of this ambiguity in Iqbal's theological output is exploring his engagement with Bradley and McTaggart.[80] Other scholars find the Qur'an as well as medieval Islamic mysticism the most pronounced historical influences on Iqbal's conception of God.[81]

Iqbal's conception of God in *The Reconstruction* has been classified as "panentheistic," and, under this rubric, his theological labour has been read as both a major philosophical achievement and a disaster. Salman Raschid's assessment is bleak. In *Iqbal's Concept of God*, he opines that "[Iqbal's] concept of God is a finite (panentheistic) one, and is arrived at largely by a superficial and uncritical reading of western science and philosophy."[82] For Raschid, Iqbal is not "a great religious thinker,"[83] and his theological output "provides virtually no original, or even independent, argumentation."[84]

For Robert Whittemore, Iqbal's theological reflections have "pointed the way to a solution of the perennial conflict between science, philosophy, and religion."[85] Iqbal's panentheistic reconstruction of Islamic theology earns him, Whittemore proposes, a rightful place in the small band of thinkers – including Whitehead, Charles Hartshorne, and Nikolai Berdyaev – who have taken up the challenge of uniting "the Absolute of cosmology with the Person of monotheism," which is "*the* problem for twentieth century philosophers."[86] For Whittemore, the "measure of Iqbal's contribution to western thought is, in large part, his success in showing that the proper understanding of the meaning and relation of religion, philosophy, and science will be attained only when men come to realize that each is only a perspective, but a perspective for the lack of which Reality would be the less."[87]

Scholars who find Iqbal's theology productive have engaged with it in various ways. For Martin Nguyen, *The Reconstruction*, along with al-Ghazālī's *Revival of the Religious Sciences*, inspires his contemporary project of "constructing a new way of understanding matters of faith."[88] For Basit Koshul, Iqbal's reflections on God in *The Reconstruction* alter classical articulations of the cosmological, ontological, and teleological arguments for God's existence, "offering an alternative that is more faithful to both empirical reality and revealed scripture."[89] Farhan Shah argues that Iqbal's panentheistic conception of God provides a springboard that can nourish contemporary "process interpretation[s] of God, the Qur'an and Islam."[90]

In his survey of the diverse reception of Iqbal's reflections on God, Yaseen Noorani suggests analyzing these thoughts for their contribution to "the general aims of Islamic modernist thinking."[91] "The overriding aim of Iqbal's writings . . . is the reform and vitalization of Muslim individuals, and by this means, of the Muslim community as a whole, and particularly the Indian Muslim community. It is necessary to understand . . . how his conception of God advances this aim."[92] In similar vein, M. Saeed Sheikh, whose annotated version of *The Reconstruction* underlies all contemporary editions of the text, insists: "Iqbal's interest in the reinterpretation of Islam in terms of modern science and philosophy is essentially and primarily of a practical nature and not merely theoretical or academic."[93]

Following the lead of scholars such as Noorani and Saeed Sheikh, I've shown in this chapter that Iqbal's argumentation about and proof of God constitute a response to a set of problems that *The Reconstruction* aims to resolve through its "philosophical test." But a significant slippage, to which I've alluded above, occurs during this process. While validating interpretive engagements with revelatory experience as a trustworthy source of knowledge claims, Iqbal criticizes foundational and descriptive conceptions of science. He criticizes the idea that physical or biological science provides unmediated access to reality and the notion that their conceptual apparatuses offer a "view of reality." In fact, the way Iqbal sets up his intellectual test, and the way he handles physics and biology as interpretations of experience, exemplify the performative and contextual aspects of his pragmatic voice. His test is squarely in the service of figuring out how an intellectual habitus might include activities simultaneously from the Islamic intellectual tradition such as scriptural interpretation and theology and from modern sciences such as physics and biology. The test exemplifies the "performative" aspect of *The Reconstruction*'s pragmatic voice. Its value lies in its capacity to address the problematic tendency K_3. *The Reconstruction* configures physics and biology as contextual interpretations of different dimensions of human experience. Their conceptual apparatuses derive their legitimacy from their capacity to examine, control, and predict a certain class of phenomena rather than propositionally mirror or describe reality.

But the minute Iqbal turns to psychology, his epistemic voice changes pitch. His claims become descriptive and foundational, are de-coupled from any context, and lose sight of a specifiable problematic situation that they might redress. Iqbal discusses psychology in the very terms he repudiates for physics and biology. In its battle against "materialism" and "mechanism," *The Reconstruction* argues that these positions are a consequence of illegitimately assuming that any discipline's theoretical apparatus yields a "view" of reality as such. But as Iqbal advocates that reality is of the character of a "centralizing ego," he takes psychological introspection as *precisely* the kind of activity that can afford a direct vision of reality. The examination of life at the level of consciousness, *The Reconstruction* tells us, yields a generic concept, an insight, available to any and all practices of knowing.

We saw in chapter 2 that *The Reconstruction* is wary of the claim that certain experiences "directly" disclose the character of reality. But this is what it does as it argues that meditation or psychological introspection forces a necessary idea upon the meditating or introspective consciousness – namely, that reality is of the character of a self. This insight is a first-hand, "direct revelation of the ultimate nature of Reality . . . [Reality] must be conceived as an ego."[94] Since this is a direct vision of reality, it yields a universal concept, descriptive of reality, unbounded by any constraints or practices of knowing: "I have conceived the Ultimate Reality as an Ego; and I must add now that from the Ultimate Ego only egos proceed . . . The world, in all its details, from the mechanical movement of what we call the atom of matter to the free movement of thought in the human ego . . . is an ego."[95]

Not atoms, not things, not space, not time, not laws, nought but selfhood (*khudi*) is the actual nature of reality. *The Reconstruction*'s "philosophical test" begins with a specific, contextual need to address a crisis-inducing intellectual tendency facing Muslim university students in India (K_3). It promises a conceptual coherence to *this* habitus, a possible *Weltbild* appropriate to the needs of its audience. Iqbal ends up constructing the only rationally conceivable world, founded on an incorrigible, direct insight into the nature of reality. Iqbal maintains that psychological introspection affords unmediated intellectual insights. On the basis of such introspection, he generates a global master category, no longer meant simply to address the questions I formalized in the epistemological, ontological, and cognitive-dissonance models of his intellectual test, but offered as a necessary view of the world.

By offering a foundationally grounded, global, and necessary view of the world, Iqbal enacts a hermeneutics of war against any set of intellectual practices that conceptualizes the phenomena it handles in different ways. Physicists, for instance, should conceptualize atoms as "egos," otherwise they inaccurately describe the atom's true nature; dendrologists should think of trees as "selves," if they are to grasp the essence of trees, and so on. In fact, any reasonable cognition should imagine that the world is composed of egos, otherwise it misreads reality and is at war with individuals, habits, and practices that grasp the "world in all its detail . . . [as] an ego."[96]

The interplay between Iqbal's representational and pragmatic epistemic voices is a little different in this chapter than in chapter 2. There I showed Iqbal's framework for relating knowledge, experience, and reality, which was pragmatic and corrected representational approaches to religion. His own arguments about religion and revelation, however, displayed the representationalist errors that his framework was designed to correct. In this chapter, we saw that Iqbal actually performs his contextual approach to knowledge in his analyses of physics and biology. But his representational voice comes to the fore as he reflects on psychological experience. As we witness in chapter 4, human selfhood is a theme where Iqbal most consistently scribes his arguments in pragmatic form.

CHAPTER FOUR

The Human Being as Self

As we just saw in chapter 3, the concept of *khudi* (selfhood) functions in *The Reconstruction* as a "master category." Everything in the universe is ultimately a "self" or a composite of various "selves." Iqbal imagines egos or selves as the basic "building blocks" of the universe: "The world, in all its details, from the mechanical movement of what we call the atom of matter to the free movement of thought in the human ego . . . is an ego."[1]

In chapter 3, I showed the role that *khudi* plays in a worldview in which the discursive resources of classical and medieval Islam can cohere with those of modern philosophy and science. The concept, we saw, is central to Iqbal's vision of an intellectual universe in which religion and science could be "at home." In this chapter, we explore Iqbal's construction of a subjectivity that can pull together the two realms: a kind of subject for whom the intellectual resources of Islam and modernity may cohere. I parse out the epistemological dimensions of Iqbal's construction of a philosophical anthropology for modern Muslim subjects.

I offer a three-part analysis of *The Reconstruction*'s style and method of constructing a philosophical anthropology. First, I give my readers a sense of the scope of scholarly reflection on Iqbal's conception of *khudi* as he applies it to human persons. Second, I consider two styles of thinking about the human person that Iqbal criticizes, one that gives it global and timeless features and one that takes subjectivity to be an epiphenomenon, decomposable to more basic elements. Third, I discuss Iqbal's own procedures for conceptualizing the human person – most notably the way he attributes freedom and immortality to it. In this part I show that Iqbal's conceptual manœuvres correct and transform the kinds of anthropologies he finds problematic.

I

Scholars have noted various intellectual-genealogical sources of Iqbal's notion of human selfhood as well as its theological, political, and philosophic import. He himself participated in heated debates about the genealogies of *khudi*. When his *Secrets of the Self* was translated into English by R.A. Nicholson in 1920, E.M. Forster and G.L. Dickinson commented on its distinctively Nietzschean ring. Forster wrote: "Iqbal completed his education in Europe . . . and like other of his compatriots he has been influenced by Nietzsche; he [Iqbal] tries to find, in that rather shaky ideal of the Superman, a guide."[2] In a letter exchange with Nicholson, Iqbal challenged the link to Nietzsche's *Übermensch*: "Some of the English reviewers," he complained, "have been misled by the superficial resemblance of some of my ideas to those of Nietzsche."[3] He suggested that a more accurate and authentic source of his notion of ego or *khudi* is the "Sufi doctrine of the Perfect Man [*al-Insān al-Kāmil*]."[4] Readers such as Forster wrongfully, he commented, conflate his reflections on human selfhood with "the German thinker's Superman [whereas] I wrote on the Sufi doctrine of the Perfect Man more than twenty years ago, long before I had read or heard anything of Nietzsche."[5]

Iqbal then alludes to one of his essays and subsequent doctoral work on Persian metaphysics, where he thematizes the notion of the complete or perfect human.[6] To Nicholson he speculates that the imagined debt to Nietzsche might derive from his own introductory notes to Nicholson's translation: "In my notes which now form part of your Introduction to [*Secrets of the Self*], I deliberately explained my position in reference to Western thinkers, as I thought this would facilitate the understanding of my views in England. I could have easily explained myself in the light of the Quran and Muslim Sufis and thinkers."[7] Iqbal also provides more useful intellectual contexts than Nietzsche; the anglophone reader, he tells Nicholson, should understand his notion of "the ideal man" in the light of John Mackenzie's *Introduction to Social Philosophy*, which he quotes:

> "There can be no ideal society without ideal man: and for production of these we require not only insight but a motive power; fire as well as light. Perhaps, a philosophic understanding of our social problems is not even the chief want of our time. We need prophets as well as teachers . . . Perhaps we want a new Christ . . . Or perhaps

our chief want is rather for the poet of the new age than for its prophet . . . [We seek a poet] who shall show us . . . the presence of the Divine in the human . . . one who shall teach us to see the working out of our highest ideals in the everyday life of the world."[8]

Iqbal suggests, for readers more conversant with the Islamic tradition, the work of medieval Muslim mystics: "I claim that the philosophy of [*Secrets of the Self*] is a direct development out of the experience and speculation of old Muslim Sufis and thinkers."[9]

Schimmel takes this avenue and discusses Iqbal's contributions to the problematics of "Islamic mystical anthropology" by noting that Iqbal's anthropological reflection "connects him with the early Persian mystics, notably with Rûmî."[10] She rejects Nietzschean sources:

> It is not difficult to interpret Iqbal's *khudî* in the light of Rûmî's teachings . . . Iqbâl's interpretation of man's situation seems to express best the seemingly contradictory ideas found in various branches of Islamic thought. Rûmî and, following him, Iqbâl have highlighted the necessity of man's working with the given facts of this world and, at the same time, developing his spiritual essence . . . to such an extent that a loving, creative dialogue between man and God becomes possible, rather, is required so that man can return from this spiritual dialogue in prayer into the world to act there according to his experience in the Divine Presence – just as the Prophet returned from his meditations in the cave of Hira, into the world to preach what had been revealed to him.[11]

Genealogical conversations on sources and influences have continued to this day. Aziz Ahmad's "Sources of Iqbal's Perfect Man" observes that Iqbal's ideal human being has "something of the Sufi mystic" and, despite Iqbal's protestations, "some 'romanesque' elements of Nietzsche's Zarathushtra,"[12] but the "philosophical structure" underlying Iqbal's *khudi* is "strongly Bergsonian."[13] Hasan Azad argues that Iqbal's ideas of selfhood "derive from a specifically modern, Western notion of the self that has its history in Rene Descartes'[s] *cogito ergo sum*."[14]

Such speculations on sources are complemented by discussions of future possibilities. The inaugural, 1952 volume of the journal *Iqbal*, published by Pakistan's Bazm-i Iqbal – a governmental institute set up to "research and [publish] on the philosophy and teachings of Iqbal"[15] – says in its editorial note that the philosopher was a "force that not only initiated a revolution in the fields of political, cultural and philosophical ideas within his own homeland, but, having crossed the boundaries of that land, is now quickening the whole of the Muslim world to a new awakening. In fact his philosophy of the Ego has become a refreshing source of inspiration for the whole of the struggling East."[16] The journal's first issues discuss Iqbal's conception of human selfhood, recount disputes about its sources, and speculate enthusiastically on its future possibilities. Mohammad Rafiuddin, an early director of Pakistan's Iqbal Academy, elevates Iqbal's notion of *khudi* (and his thought more broadly) to world-historic proportions. The idea of the self is the crowning concept in Iqbal's thought, the "intellectual king" of a "future world-state which will endure for ever."[17]

Scholars have thematized the theological dimensions of Iqbal's reflection on human personhood as well. Schimmel observes that Iqbal's *khudi*, like his thought in general, reflects a heroic attempt to breathe life into the "deteriorated" body of Islam in India, where life "was spent mostly in the blind acceptance of accustomed symbols."[18] "Iqbal's anthropology, the whole concept of *khūdī*, of development of Self is understandable only in the larger context of his theology. What [Iqbal] aims at, is . . . [the human person as] a being that grows the more perfect the closer his connection with God is."[19] For Schimmel, *khudi* articulates relations between human beings and God, setting up nearness and proximity with God as the measure of human achievement: "In Iqbal's anthropology that man is greatest who has realized his self in relation to God . . . i.e. who is nearest to God in creativity and activity."[20] For Ebrahim Moosa, Iqbal "urge[s] Muslims to find the optimal set of ideas for the human condition as experienced in his day."[21] Moosa notes that the "human person in Iqbal's view is a sentient, believing, and ethical being . . . [who] only triumphs through love of the divine."[22]

For Sheila McDonough, Iqbal's notion of *khudi* configures "I–Thou" rather than "I–It" relations between human beings and God.[23] Iqbal, she writes, by configuring "I–Thou" relations between human beings and God, structures a metaphysical outlook that lends epistemological humility to humans' theological claims: "To conceive of God as most like a person is to insist that God cannot be the object of human manipulation. Another is someone who can be heard and responded to, but not controlled."[24] Theological claims cannot be uttered with "perfect clarity"[25] because God is not an "object" or an "it" for an inquirer to map and control by epistemic machinations and desires. For McDonough, *khudi* constructs an epistemic environment in which to seek knowledge is like conversing with what one knows. It also constrains humans' claims about each other: "I–Thou" relations between persons prevent perfectly clear and totalizing descriptions of the human subject.[26]

Naveeda Khan, exploring projects of self-fashioning, striving, and self-correction that define the horizons of contemporary Pakistani identities, also notes the theological dimensions of Iqbal's *khudi*: "[For Iqbal, the] human toils with God to forge himself or herself as an individual . . . Given that this self arcs toward God and partners with God in order to advance, its self-advancement implies change in the world. In other words, the creation of the self and that of the world are crucially linked."[27]

Another strand of scholarly labour explores how Iqbal's notion of *khudi* relates to political questions and inquiries.[28] Iqbal Singh Sevea writes that "*khudi* (self-affirmation, or ego)" [29] and "*bekhudi* . . . the force that brings the individual ego in line with the social ego"[30] function as a conceptual fulcrum for Iqbal's critique of modern conceptions of individuality and the nation-state. For Sevea, Iqbal develops his conception of human subjectivity to criticize both the conceptual excesses of individualism and "homogenizing" ways of thinking about the nation-state. I read Sevea as arguing that, for Iqbal, human beings are not simply atomistic individuals whose cooperation creates society; nor simply functions or effects of sociality. Rejecting atomistic individuality and non-individuated sociality, Iqbal takes the paired relation between individuality and sociality as the moorings of the political habitus wherein human persons come into being.[31]

For Yaseen Noorani, Iqbal's "distinctive figuration of the human condition" grounds his "critique of Europe's rationalist and capitalist social order."[32] Iqbal posits a "desiring self" that embodies a "creative mode of being"[33] to articulate a potential trajectory for a modern Muslim subject who can transform "the earth into heaven and humanity into divinity."[34] Iqbal's desiring and striving self resists the "empiricist, calculative approach of Enlightenment rationality."[35] Such rationality constructs a human whose goal is to "possess and accumulate the objects of the world," which conception of the human furthers the exploitative and tyrannical projects of "capitalism and colonialism."[36]

Javed Majeed, who also notes the political valence of Iqbal's conception of *khudi*, argues that Iqbal defines it against "the oppressive clichés of colonial ideologies in British India, for which Indians were members of groups defined by religion and caste, and not individuals in their own right . . . Iqbal's conception of selfhood is an attempt to reconstruct, on behalf of Indian Muslims in particular . . . a counter agency to the systematic negation of the humanity of the colonized subject by European colonialism."[37]

This sampling of the genealogical, philosophical, theological, and political valence of Iqbal's notion of *khudi* confirms Shahab Ahmed's claim that Iqbal's reflections on *khudi* are a significant site of vibrant thematizations in Islamic intellectual history of "the Self as locus for the Truth and Meaning of Islam."[38] When "we think of Islam," Ahmed argues, "we should concomitantly think of the meaningful exploration of the *self* with its associated components of self-awareness, of personhood, of identity, of the individual, of the collective, of the personality, of self-action."[39]

My analysis in the rest of this chapter complements the remarkable and patient work of the scholars I have just named. It does not aim to furnish a single or even multiple accounts of Iqbal's anthropology in *The Reconstruction*. Rather, the next, second section outlines the epistemological norms Iqbal shuns as dead ends, and the third parses out the ones he puts into practice as he thematizes human subjectivity in the text.

II

Iqbal criticizes two broad styles of thinking about the human subject. The first takes subjectivity to be an epiphenomenon, decomposable to more basic and primary things. The second – outlined further below in this section – attributes global, essential, and self-consistent features to human beings.

The Reconstruction criticizes conversations about human persons that divide one's analytical universe into two parts and then takes one of the two parts as primary, causal, and basic and the other as secondary, caused, and derivative. I'm going to present two specific instances of *The Reconstruction*'s criticisms of analytical universes that are constructed in this fashion. The first conceives of the "human person" as an epiphenomenon (secondary, caused, derivative) reducible to or explicable in terms of the "environment" (primary, causal, basic). The other takes either "mind" or "body" as primary, causal, and basic and the other as secondary, caused, and derivative.

About approaches to human personhood that reduce subjectivity to environmental phenomena, Iqbal says: "Even if we regard the basis of soul-life[40] as purely physical, it by no means follows that the emergent can be resolved into what has conditioned its birth and growth. The emergent . . . is an unforeseeable and novel fact on its own plane of being, and cannot be explained mechanistically."[41] Atomizing and decomposing the human subject into antecedent factors or "ingredients" is reductive. It implies that any given complex thing is a sum of its parts rather than being a novel thing. It imagines that human persons are adequately describable in terms of and determined by antecedent practices and factors. Iqbal avers that this analysis gives a lop-sided account of the relationship between human beings and their environments.

He locates this same analytical gesture in mind-body analyses of the human person.[42] Such views, he insists, either privilege the mind as an independent reality and cast the body as epiphenomenally dependent on it or vice versa. Even "interactionism" between mind and body cannot explain how two such independent things end up interacting.[43] If we posit some kind of relation between the two, while taking one of them to be primary, insuperable problems arise, such as: Is the "soul . . . an organ of the body which exploits it for physiological purposes, or [is] the body . . . an instrument of the soul[?]"[44]

Iqbal offers two correctives to this particular style of thinking about the human person. First, he stresses that anthropologies should not offer unqualified, causal pictures of how humans relate to their environments. He notes that "the causal chain" in which human persons are placed by such accounts is itself a "construction" at the disposal of human beings for their "own purposes": "the *causal chain* wherein we try to find a place for the ego is itself an artificial construction of the ego for its own *purposes*. The ego is called upon to live in a complex environment, and he cannot maintain his life in it without reducing it to a system which would give him some kind of assurance as to the behaviour of things around him. The view of his environment as a system of cause and effect is thus an indispensable instrument of the ego."[45]

Iqbal cautions that inquirers, as they relate elements of an analytic universe, should not think of causality in purely descriptive terms.

Inquirers who so link persons and their environments must gesture towards their methods and purposes. In this view, causal accounts are connected to the interests of the inquirer, who, through some method, and for some purpose, parses out a complex phenomenon using an analytical scheme.

I've used a thought experiment in classrooms to illustrate Iqbal's approach to causal descriptions about human persons. I ask students to imagine two persons in different automobiles who become involved in an accident on the road. This sort of interaction can be parsed out using the analytical vocabularies of physics (Was the road slipperier than usual? How fast were the vehicles going?), economics (How does this accident affect parties' household incomes? Do cheap automobiles contribute to more frequent accidents?) biology (Was either driver impaired in some way? What kind of injuries did the two suffer?), and so on. The point of the exercise is to clarify that potential answers to questions such as "What caused this accident to happen?" or "What consequences will this accident, in turn, cause?" are connected to and articulated in terms of the disciplines, methods, and purposes that an inquirer brings to the table.

In his second corrective to the epiphenomenal approach, Iqbal suggests not treating human persons as dependent on and epiphenomenal with respect to their environments but viewing persons and their environments as distinct and co-dependent: "I am distinct from and yet intimately related to that on which I depend for my life and sustenance."[46] Indicating this sort of interdependence, Iqbal notes that "streams of causality flow into [the ego] from Nature and from it to Nature."[47] This way of configuring human persons as "*distinct*, though not *isolated*"[48] from their environments mutually implicates both participants.

Nicholas Adams and Wilfred Cantwell Smith have developed vocabularies for illuminating such contexts of "mutual implication" – "pair" relations (Adams) and "bilateral" terms (Smith). Adams's notion of pairs is meant to clarify relations between two things (e.g., humans and environments; mind and body), where treating the two as independent, and then relating them as primary–secondary, causal–caused; and basic–derivative does not work well.[49]

Adams attributes three features to his notion of pairs. First, "a pair is not two things that happen to be in relation. *A pair is two things, where each is what it is because of its relation to the other.*"[50] Second, "a pair is not one thing with two parts. *A pair is two things, where each is distinct from the other, but each cannot be adequately described independently of its relation to the other.* One can describe each of the persons who has been married for twenty years, and it is not a mistake to try to describe just one of them. An adequate description of that one, however, will involve some account of his/her relation to the spouse – the other, and also some account of his/her being as a married person."[51] Third, discussions about paired terms have three parts, involving the two terms along with their relation: "In the case of the married couple," Adams continues, "there is the husband, the wife, and their relation in marriage."[52]

Similarly, Smith proposes "bilateral terms" to clarify relationships in which the "partners" are reciprocally and evenly implicated. Smith's flagship example is that of scripture: "'Scripture' is a bilateral term. By that we mean that it inherently implies, in fact names, a relationship ... No person is a husband in and of himself; he is a husband in correlation with another person ... No one is a king except in relation to a certain society and form of government; no building is a temple except in relation to a given community of persons ... [Similarly] no text is a scripture in itself and as such."[53]

Both Adams and Smith's notions illuminate the way *The Reconstruction* recalibrates approaches that reduce reciprocal relations to epiphenomenal terms. My discussion of the way Iqbal handles the relationship between human persons and their environments in *The Reconstruction* is also complemented by Sevea's observation that, for Iqbal, individuality (selfness; *khudi*) and sociality (selflessness; *bekhudi*) function in tandem with each other.[54]

The second style of looking at human beings that Iqbal criticizes is the search for global, essential, and self-consistent features. He takes currents in classical and medieval Islamic philosophy and theology that think of the human ego in terms of a "simple, indivisible, and immutable soul-substance"[55] as an occasion for criticizing such approaches and offers two avenues of correction. First, anthropologies ought to be conceived as time-specific and tied to the needs and context of a community. In a letter to Sahibzada Aftab Ahmad Khan, vice-chancellor of Aligarh Muslim University, about syllabi for religious subjects, Iqbal observes: "The spiritual needs of a community change with the expansion of that community's outlook on life. The change in the position of the individual, his intellectual liberation and infinite advance in natural sciences have entirely changed the substance of modern life so that the kind of scholasticism or theological thought which satisfied a Muslim in the Middle Ages would not satisfy him today."[56]

Global and timeless claims about human persons lack the flexibility to "satisfy" and address the questions and concerns of historically and geographically extended communities. For Iqbal, scholastic or metaphysical reflection (cosmological, anthropological, eschatological, and so on) becomes less responsive over time to the "spiritual needs of a community" as they transform. *The Reconstruction* insists that "a practically dead metaphysics" cannot "be of any help to those who happen to possess a different intellectual background."[57] Moosa comments that Iqbal realized "that the lived conditions of each epoch generated their own founding myths and metaphysics"[58] and that "Muslim mystics, philosophers, and the pious in every age forged a notion of the self."[59]

Second, Iqbal takes issue with such approaches because they posit a consistent set of predicates as the essence that operates "behind the scenes" to unify and cohere human action.[60] He considers such essences as at best "formal conditions," not as some sort of thing or "substance": "Kant's fallacies of pure reason are well known to the student of modern philosophy. The 'I think', which accompanies every thought is, according to Kant, a purely formal condition of thought, and the transition from a purely formal condition of thought to ontological substance is logically illegitimate."[61]

Nicholas Adams has a delightful way of clarifying Kant's distinction between constitutive things and regulative ideals. In an omelette, he tells us, the eggs are constitutive, but the idea of a perfect omelette, which guides the practice of its construction, is a regulative ideal.[62] I am building on Adams's analogy to say that the recipe or instructions for making omelettes are the formal conditions for bringing about omelettes in the world. Such formal conditions are not the same kind of thing as the omelette's ingredients. For Iqbal, thinkers who, to explain how humans are "unified," ascribe some kind of behind-the-scenes essence to them are offering at most formal conditions, not substances or essences.

More gravely, any account of formal or transcendental conditions tied to a thing (such as an omelette) is stimulated by patterns observed in experience. Uniformly well-cooked omelettes can, for example, suggest there are patterned formal conditions (recipes, cookbooks) that bring about such a dish. But essential accounts of the kind Iqbal is castigating do not handle the variety, multiplicity, and many-sidedness of human beings well and are not borne out by observation or experience.[63]

Given Iqbal's attack on epiphenomenal or timeless and self-consistent accounts, how does he observe and attribute human characteristics? In the next section, I show his epistemological style vis-à-vis human beings in the *Reconstruction*, based on cenoscopy, probability, and aspiration.

III

Iqbal claims that "the human ego" is free. As he convinces his readers of this claim, he does not construct an ontology or picture of humanness and thence tease out or deduce the notion of freedom. Instead he applies a procedure akin to what philosophers such as Jeremy Bentham, Charles Peirce, and John Deely refer to as "cenoscopy,"[64] or cœnoscopy (from the Greek *koinos*, or common): the study of the everyday world. There are two kinds of things that cenoscopically shaped arguments may not do. First, they may not exclusively rely on the kinds of observations accessible to experts in controlled experimental environments that require specialized equipment, such as microscopes or test-tubes. Second, they should not require their audience to be fully conversant with the technical vocabulary of a particular discipline such as physics or economics.

These principles mean that cenoscopic arguments rely on evidence, observations, and concepts that are *readily available* to the claimant and their audience.[65] So how does *The Reconstruction*'s cenoscopic style attribute freedom to human persons? Iqbal gestures towards ideas, sources, patterns, events, or facts that his readers can conceptualize, refer to, practise, and observe *as a matter of course* and uses such evidence as a reliable means of claiming that human beings can be conceived as free. Specifically, with respect to freedom, it is as if *The Reconstruction* asks its readers if they, during the course of their lives, make future plans. Do they, for instance, plan on Sunday night that they're going to wake up on Monday and make an omelette for breakfast? And does the future pan out according to their plans? If so, Iqbal says that he and his readers have enough warrant to attribute the feature of freedom to their persons.

Freedom is *The Reconstruction*'s name for the following set of phenomena: the readers of this text, as a matter of course, envision future possibilities, which, in light of purposive action, end up being enacted: "It is [the] sense of striving in the experience of purposive action and *the success which I actually achieve in reaching my 'ends'* that convinces me of my efficiency as a personal cause."[66]

"But, surely," readers might retort, "there are a fair few instances where we pursue a specific vision of the future but events do not consistently pan out in accordance with our desires." *The Reconstruction* responds that "the power to act freely"[67] is not a consistent feature of a given person's everyday life. Both freedom and its absence might be evinced in the course of a person's day. Some of their plans might come to fruition, just as they imagined, others may suffer modification, and others yet might be thwarted. The modality of Iqbal's attribution of freedom to human persons, then, is not necessary but probabilistic.

The Reconstruction seems to be claiming that those who observe human persons are likely to observe that people make plans, which come to fruition, but such fruition is not necessary. Those observers will also see that some plans do not come to fruition. This kind of probabilistic claim, which is also offered in relation to situations such as the weather, or the potential outcome of a football match, or the location of sub-atomic particles, is not a "poorer cousin" of necessary claims. Probabilistic claims are appropriate to situations that are uncertain and ambiguous. *The Reconstruction*'s probabilistic style of attributing freedom to humans – by admitting that its absence will also be visible in their activities – tries to be appropriate to the ambiguities, contradictions, and uncertainties that characterize human lives.

But readers might still retort, "Do you mean to say that, if I were to 'add up' all my plans for the day, week, or year, I'm going to discover that what I intend to pursue takes place more than 50 or 60 per cent of the time? And if it turns out, as I quantify my experiences, that, on a good day, only 30 per cent of my plans come to pass, wouldn't you say that I'm unfree rather than free?"

This line of inquiry would elicit the third and final style that Iqbal adopts vis-à-vis human characteristics. Simply put, as *The Reconstruction* attributes features to human beings, it offers them as cenoscopically verified, probabilistically observable, *aspirations*, or objects of continual pursuit. It does not offer such features as "naturally occurring" properties. Recall Nicholas Adams's account of omelettes. Making them requires ingredients such as eggs and salt, formal conditions and rules such as recipes or cookbooks, and goals that guide the practice, such as "deliciousness." Objects of pursuit that regulate or guide practice are usually identifiable as habits or patterns in a given practice and not isolatable and specifiable in the same way that one may identify eggs and cooking utensils.

For instance, if a given set of practices is guided by the pursuit of health, this object (health; healthiness) will be identifiable as a habit or pattern performed in a whole series of practices, such as waking up at a consistent time in the morning, sleeping for 7–8 hours at night, exercising, regulating one's diet a certain way, and so on.[68] Health would be identifiable as a goal or aspiration that is fulfilled (or not) in the performance of a set of practices. Furthermore, since it is an embodied habit, its pursuit would have to be maintained or enacted continuously or indefinitely; the habits and patterns that constitute healthiness are displayed in a given person's life insofar as that person continuously pursues healthiness. Stated differently, the habits or patterns that guide the shape of a practice have their being in the continual pursuit of the goal or aspiration towards which they aim. In this vein, Iqbal's attribution of freedom to human persons is the attribution of an aspiration or goal for them to perform, cultivate, and embody, not a descriptive property of persons. One who attributes features to humans offers an account of what they ought to pursue as ideals of indefinite pursuit.

Iqbal's style of predicating "freedom" as a goal to aspire to is exemplified in his discussion of the function of prayer in *The Reconstruction*: "Islam recognizes a very important fact of human psychology, i.e. the rise and fall of the power to act freely, and is anxious to retain the power to act freely as a constant and undiminished factor in the life of the ego. The timing of the daily prayer, which, according to the Qur'an, restores 'self-possession' to the ego . . . is intended to save the ego from the mechanizing effects of sleep and business. Prayer in Islam is the ego's escape from mechanism to freedom."[69]

The aspirational aspect of Iqbal's style of talking about human beings is thematized in detail by Naveeda Khan and Shahab Ahmed. They note that, for Iqbal, Muslims are implicated in projects of forging and crafting themselves, as they explore the meaning and valence of their lives in relation to theo-political, historical, and revelatory horizons.[70] Khan writes, for instance, that Iqbal delineates paths of "Muslim aspiration without asserting a final end to striving."[71] Sevea comments that Iqbal's "philosophy and religious thought [are] centred upon his construction of a *khudi* . . . which continually strove for its development and self-affirmation."[72]

In brief, I've argued that as Iqbal attributes features to human persons in *The Reconstruction*:

- He gives epistemological heft to experiences and observations available as a matter of course to his audience.
- He presents his claims as probabilistic. His probabilistic attribution of freedom to human beings – admitting that its absence will also be visible in their activities – responds to the ambiguities, contradictions, and uncertainties that characterize human lives.
- He shapes his predicative claims in aspirational terms, as a goal to pursue or a habit or pattern to enact in life, rather than as simply a probabilistic description of what humans are. *The Reconstruction* avers that any description of humans involves purposive concerns. Humans cannot be described without reference to their projects of fashioning, cultivating, and forming themselves.

As I close this chapter, I corroborate my case by showing how Iqbal's attribution of "immortality" to human persons also exemplifies these three features. In making cenoscopic claims about immortality, Iqbal draws on couplets by Rumi to claim that human beings are connected with their surrounding environment. They have come into being out of "inorganic things" and then moved through "vegetative to the animal state," and thereafter "the great Creator . . . drew man out of the animal into the human state . . . And he will be again changed from his present soul."[73] The question of immortality is "not a problem to be decided by arguments of [a] purely metaphysical nature."[74] It is to be resolved by paying attention to how human beings are connected with and evolve out of the world around them: "It is highly improbable that a being whose evolution has taken millions of years should be thrown away as a thing of no use."[75] "In view of the past history of man," Iqbal writes, referring to how human beings evolve out of inorganic and organic things, "it is highly improbable that his career should come to an end with the dissolution of his body."[76] As you can see, Iqbal's claim that humans are "immortal" is offered in cenoscopic and probabilistic terms.

But, alongside, Iqbal's speaks in aspirational terms: "Personal immortality . . . is not ours as of right; it is to be achieved by personal effort. Man is only a candidate for it."[77] Immortality is an object of pursuit and struggle: "The ego must continue to struggle until he is able to gather himself up, and win his resurrection."[78] Commenting on the way Iqbal attributes immortality to human persons in *The Reconstruction*, Christopher McClure notes: "Iqbal . . . offers an interpretation of immortality that relies on post-Einsteinian physics, is non-metaphysical but teleological, and is ambiguous enough to remain open to individual interpretation and creativity. His goal in doing so is to provide an interpretation of Islam that is more believable, and that can serve as the basis of shared meaning for Muslims in a liberal age."[79]

As I've said above, Iqbal's reflections on human selfhood are most consistently pragmatic. He employs contextual evidence, shapes his arguments in probabilistic terms, and insists that articulations of human personhood ought to be performative. Iqbal talks about human persons in cenoscopic, probabilistic, and aspirational ways to correct anthropologies that thematize them in essential, self-consistent, and purely descriptive terms. Accounts of human personhood informed by the latter three patterns cannot respond to the historical and epistemological contexts of their readers. Iqbal's corrections allow modern Muslim subjects to offer accounts of themselves that may differ from anthropological accounts authorized by medieval and classical Islamic intellectual traditions. But such difference is mediated by *The Reconstruction*'s insistence that accounts of personhood should be context-specific and appropriate to the everyday experience, ambiguities, and aspirations of the persons such accounts are offered about.

In the following chapter, we return to the more familiar pattern of Iqbal's repetition and correction of representationalism. We see that his conceptual manœuvres in relation to positions that delegitimate Muhammad's prophetic experience are polemical, apologetic, and corrective.

CHAPTER FIVE

The Meaning of Revelation

Chapters 3 and 4 proposed that the concept of *khudi* fills several roles in *The Reconstruction*. I stated initially that its pragmatic function is to rectify a tendency in the intellectual habitus of Iqbal's audience – namely, to imagine that the resources of Islamic intellectual culture are at odds with the intellectual heritage of the west. By describing knowledge as a means of establishing relationships with God's self, Iqbal argued that investigation of empirical experience and study of scriptural texts were commensurate activities. Qur'anic interpretation predicates to reality the same or commensurate features as do physics, biology, and psychology – embodiments of various "regions" or "levels" of human experience. This reality is best understood as "a rationally directed creative life,"[1] in which "thought, life, and purpose interpenetrate to form . . . the unity of a self – an all-embracing concrete self – the ultimate source of all individual life and thought."[2] This concrete self is the ultimate referent signified through the knowledge claims that emerge from various experiential contexts. Science is akin to worship, Iqbal argued, and religion is akin to patient and systematic empirical investigation of reality. This procedure, he explained, was sufficient warrant for convincing someone who is sceptical of the capacity of revelation to yield knowledge claims to envisage revelatory claims as truth-bearing.

This chapter traces Iqbal's reasoning as he shows *how* revelatory experience may become significant, referential, and truth-bearing. He seeks to display how the Qur'an (or what Iqbal calls Muhammad's revelatory experience) may achieve that status and function as a potentially formative and authoritative feature of the intellectual universe of *The Reconstruction*'s audience. I analyze Iqbal's case through two avenues.

The first examines Iqbal's practice of attributing features to Islam and Muslim culture.[3] I show that *The Reconstruction* characterizes Islam in three ways. First, Iqbal offers his claims as binary, combative descriptions of the "spirit of Islam," in competition with other such depictions. Second, he conceptualizes Islam as a vague phenomenon, about which he makes non-binary and contradictory claims. Finally, he offers his claims in an attempt to transform the rules of predicating features to Islam operative in his context.

In the second section, I discuss *The Reconstruction*'s scriptural hermeneutics. I show that Iqbal tends to read scriptural claims in two ways – as descriptive propositions, meaningful if they correspond to a particular state of affairs, and contextually, as claims whose meanings are a function of some habit of interpretation. My chief concern is to reveal how representational and pragmatic tendencies variously inform Iqbal's attempt to prove prophetic revelation meaningful as he characterizes Islam and interprets scripture.

I

Iqbal begins his discussion of the "ruling concepts of Muslim culture" in the fifth chapter of *The Reconstruction* by adducing a set of phenomena that his readers would readily admit as an observable element of their universe. He then interprets the word *waḥī* (mystical experience) in the Qur'an as a way to handle those phenomena:

> The way in which the word *Wahy* (inspiration) is used in the Qur'an, shows that the Qur'an regards it as a universal property of life; though its nature and character are different at different stages of the evolution of life. The plant growing freely in space, the animal developing a new organ to suit a new environment, and a human being receiving light from the inner depths of life, are all cases of inspiration [i.e., *waḥī*] varying in character according to the needs of the recipient, or the needs of the species to which the recipient belongs.[4]

The Reconstruction sets up the stage for arguing the meaningfulness of scripture or prophetic revelation by claiming that, apart from other usages, the Qur'an uses the word *waḥī* to name: "animal[s] developing a new organ to suit a new environment"; plants being "able to grow"; human beings getting "inspired" in moments of need.[5] These are the kinds of things that Iqbal's readers would readily admit as observable elements of their experience: animals evolving, plants growing, human beings finding inspiration in times of need and so on. Iqbal's next move is to state that the Qur'an applies the word *waḥī* to such commonplace phenomena. This move warrants readers to not look at *waḥī* askance, as something outlandish or unfamiliar. It's a "disarming" gesture that refers the term *waḥī* to things Iqbal's readers would consider familiar and customary.

As we discussed in chapter 2, Iqbal is writing in a context where thinkers refer religion to either subjectivity or primitive forms of objectivity. I argued in chapter 3 that *The Reconstruction* perceives such approaches – embodied in the educational apparatuses of the British Empire – as producing a crisis among young Muslims studying there. Such students are being trained in habits of thought that make ideas such as revelation, prophecy, and God inconceivable, frame the intellectual heritage of Islam and the west as competing, and delegitimate commensurate relationships between religion and science. There is evidence to suggest that Iqbal speaks here not just as a university instructor and functionary of colonial educational, political, and legal institutions, but as the kind of young student whom he addresses in *The Reconstruction*, who wrestles with the potentially alienating and "de-muslimizing"[6] consequences of imperial education.

Iqbal attended the Scotch Mission School in Sialkot because one of his teachers, Mir Hasan, convinced Iqbal's father to place him in an English school.[7] Iqbal also speaks as a graduate of the Government College in Lahore, Cambridge University, and the Ludwig Maximilian University of Munich. His reflections on his time at these institutions reveal his sense of how they generate styles of discourse that systematically negate and marginalize the traditions of thought and practice of the colonized, while elevating the empire's.

In his biography of Iqbal, Javed Iqbal recounts his father's personal encounter with such styles of discourse. During one of his summer breaks in England, Iqbal went with a Scottish friend to the latter's hometown. A few days into his stay, Iqbal found out that missionaries just back from India were scheduled to give a public lecture on their activities there. Iqbal and his friend went to the event, which had attracted a huge crowd, and heard: "There are 300 million people in India, but it wouldn't be accurate to refer to them as people. In their habits, attributes, and customs they are considerably inferior to humans and a little better than animals. We have, even after years of struggle, only barely introduced these animal-like humans to civilization."[8]

After the lecture, Iqbal was moved to give a twenty-five-minute rejoinder, denouncing the way the missionaries chose to conceptualize, understand, and relate with Indians:[9] "Look at my face, my skin, my clothes, my comportment," said Iqbal, as if to recover his humanity, "and you can estimate for yourself the degree to which what the missionaries just said about Indians is accurate."[10] The missionaries' style of predication *delegitimates* what this style purportedly seeks to understand by predicating "animality," "inferiority," "incivility" to Indians.

The Reconstruction avers that such a delegitimating logic of predication is at work as colonial pedagogical institutions and scholars make claims about Islam, Muhammad, and the Qur'an. In his most fervent and fiery comments on such styles of predication, which delegitimate Muhammad's revelatory claims as truth-bearing, Iqbal alludes to scholars such as D.B. MacDonald,[11] Margoliouth,[12] and Nicholson[13] and writes:

> Muhammad, we are told, was a psychopath. Well, if a psychopath has the power to give a fresh direction to the course of human history, it is a point of the highest psychological interest to search his original experience which has turned slaves into leaders of men, and has inspired the conduct and shaped the career of whole races of mankind. Judging from the various types of activity that emanated from the movement initiated by the Prophet of Islam, his spiritual tension and the kind of behaviour which issued from it, cannot be regarded as a response to a mere fantasy inside his brain.[14]

This is a retort to claims such as MacDonald's, who, in his analysis of traditions that record Muhammad's religious experiences, observes: "What is certain is the existence of some pathological condition in Muḥammad, resulting in trances, and it is not at all impossible that Sprenger's judgment . . . that it was some form of hysteria under which he suffered, may be correct. A more detailed examination in the light of the recent investigations of nervous diseases through hypnotism might reach more sure results."[15]

Genealogical inquiries into revelatory claims discredit them as "fantastic," "pathological," and a form of "nervous disease." In such an environment, *The Reconstruction* suggests examining and paying attention to the *consequences* of prophetic claims to revelation to discover their meaning.[16] It suggests assessing the rationality and meaning of Prophets' revelatory claims by examining "the cultural world that [springs out of the spirit of a prophet's] message."[17]

Iqbal's suggestion in *The Reconstruction* for understanding and engaging with prophetic claims resembles what he recommended to a reader, Ṣāliḥ Muḥammad, who sought to write a translation of Iqbal's *Payām-i Mashriq*. While he was preparing his translation, Iqbal wrote to him: "You should not consult me. You should try to candidly and clearly express the way my couplets affect your heart. Inquiring after the author's intentions is entirely unnecessary, and, in fact, detrimental . . . The same couplet affects different hearts differently. In fact [it affects the same heart] differently on different occasions . . . If a couplet produces different effects on different hearts, it is evidence of the power and life of the couplet."[18]

To judge the meaning or the "power and life" of prophetic revelation is to look into the "various types of activity" that "emanate" from one who claims to be a Prophet: "The prophet's [religious experience] is creative . . . The desire to see his religious experience transformed into a living world-force is supreme in the prophet. Thus his return [from *waḥī*] amounts to a kind of pragmatic test of the value of his religious experience . . . [a] way of judging the value of a prophet's religious experience, therefore, would be to examine the type of manhood that he has created, and the cultural world that has sprung out of the spirit of his message."[19]

This conceptual move, i.e., analyzing the consequences rather than the genesis of what purports to be revelatory, is Iqbal's signature attempt to transform the way colonial scholarship predicates features to Islam, Muhammad, and the Qur'an. It is prompted by analyses that treat revelatory claims as epistemologically empty traces of biological disease.[20]

As I stated in the opening pages of this chapter, Iqbal predicates features to Islam in three forms: combative, binary descriptions of its "spirit"; contradictory claims that treat it as a vague phenomenon; and rules for transforming how colonial scholars conceptualize it. These three forms have elicited three corresponding styles of reading from *The Reconstruction*'s interpreters, which I illustrate through Tayob (A), Diagne (B), and Majeed (C).

Tayob (style A) notes that Iqbal, like other modernists, attempts to capture the "spirit" or "essence" of Islam in an attempt to "save Muslims from the doubts and critique that came with modernity."[21] Tayob writes that Muslim modernists' "considered reflections on the essence of religion . . . provided them with an apparently permanent core at the heart of Islam. And they argued that this core was clearly present from the beginning of Islam . . . They [posit] religion and Islam as stable centres in a bewildering and fast-changing world."[22]

In this reading, Iqbal's practice of predication aims to isolate something elemental and incorrigible from the vast expanse of the history of Islam and posit it as the religion's "permanent core." The function of this "extra-historical" core is to protect Islam from the political, epistemological, and moral "ravages of modernity."[23] In this style of reading (A), *The Reconstruction* attributes self-consistent, foundational, and a-historical predicates to Islam.[24]

Diagne (style B), in contrast, regards Iqbal's treatment of Islam as vague. *The Reconstruction*'s attempt to articulate the spirit of Islam is not meant, he says, to secure a stable, a-historical essence but emphasizes movement, fidelity, permanence, change, dynamism, and conservatism as features that constitute Islam. Iqbal's "ethos" of Islam involves "a process of continuous creation, of permanent innovation and emergence, which prevent the intention of religion becoming imprisoned within reasonings . . . claiming a 'final character.'"[25]

For Diagne, Iqbal conceptualizes Islam in multifarious and contradictory ways, or what Shahab Ahmed calls "coherent contradictions."[26] In this reading *The Reconstruction* attributes contradictory predicates to the object of its analysis (i.e., Islam). It takes Islam to be "in the making" and therefore not the kind of object about which fully stable and self-consistent claims can be authorized.[27]

Majeed (style C) argues that Iqbal's work on Islam aims not to describe it but to transform and correct how it is constructed as an object of inquiry in the context of colonial modernity.[28]

There is ample evidence in *The Reconstruction* to warrant each of these styles of reading. Styles like Tayob's are warranted by the volume's efforts to distill Islam's "essence" from historical "distortions," as in Iqbal's comments on the "finality of the institution of prophethood"[29] and his arguments that "the spirit of Muslim culture . . . for purposes of knowledge . . . fixes its gaze on the concrete, the finite."[30] The finality of prophethood, Iqbal argues, means that "mystic experience . . . however unusual or abnormal, must now be regarded by a Muslim as a perfectly natural experience, open to critical scrutiny like other aspects of human experience."[31] For Iqbal, this idea opens up all avenues of human experience as potential sources of knowledge. Just as the proclamation that there is no god but God divests "the forces of Nature of that Divine character with which earlier cultures had clothed them,"[32] the finality of prophethood divests all facets of "inner experience" of supernatural authority: "The intellectual value of the idea is that it tends to create an independent critical attitude towards mystic experience by generating the belief that all personal authority, claiming a supernatural origin, has come to an end in the history of man."[33]

Concomitant to this idea of finality for Iqbal is the idea of "the birth of inductive intellect."[34] Muslim intellectual culture – which developed out of sustained contact with, reflection on, and appropriation of Greek intellectual traditions – came into "its own," he believes, through a slow "revolt" against Greek philosophy.[35] Iqbal argues that, for Greek philosophy, broadly speaking, acquiring knowledge "elevates" the seeker from the observable to the theoretical. He cites examples from classical and medieval Islamic culture – Ibn Taymiyyah's critique of Greek logic, Ash'arite atomism and occasionalism, and al-Khwārazmī's number as "pure relation" rather than pure magnitude – to argue that "authentic" classical and medieval Muslim intellectual culture is anti-classical:[36] "For purposes of knowledge, it fixes its gaze on the concrete, the finite . . . Knowledge must begin with the concrete. It is the intellectual capture of and *power* over the concrete that makes it possible for the intellect of man to pass beyond the concrete."[37]

Iqbal claims that the various sciences of classical and medieval Islam were built on ontologies and metaphysical conceptions that revolted against the "ruling concepts" of eternal fixity and proportion. In kinship with pragmatic critiques, especially in Dewey's *Reconstruction in Philosophy*, Iqbal argues that Greek metaphysics cherishes speculation, immutable certainty, and a fixed universe.[38] Iqbal's genealogical claim is that "authentic" Islamic reflection on the Qur'an challenged the intellectual ideals of immutable certainty and fixity: "The ideal of the Greeks . . . was proportion, not infinity . . . In the history of Muslim culture, on the other hand, we find that both in the realms of pure intellect and religious psychology, by which term I mean higher Sufism, the ideal revealed is the possession and enjoyment of the Infinite."[39]

In analyzing the finality of prophethood and the anti-classical bent of Islamic intellectual culture – as Tayob (style A) rightly notes – Iqbal seeks some way to identify "genuinely" Islamic ideas. Insofar as Muslim intellectuals build on, rather than criticizing and amending Greek philosophical assumptions, they betray, for Iqbal, the Qur'an's anti-classical spirit and obfuscate its message.[40] It is a "misunderstanding that Greek thought, in any way, determined the character of Muslim culture."[41] In contrast to Greek thought, authentic Muslim intellectual culture valorized the "concrete," and gave birth to inductive, experimental, and scientific methods of exploring reality.[42]

Iqbal displays even more clearly this tendency to seek Islam's essence in his general assertions about the nature of the Qur'an and Islam in "Islam as a Moral and Political Ideal." He writes, for instance, that there is no such thing as slavery in Islam;[43] that all the Prophet's wars were a form of defensive *jihad*;[44] and that "Islam is a religion of peace."[45] Style A of reading Iqbal, à la Tayob, is legitimated where *The Reconstruction* offers counter-polemical, descriptive predicates about the Qur'an or Islam against the kinds of "colonial" scholarship of MacDonald, Margoliouth, and Nicholson seen above. If such writings portray a violent and bloodthirsty religion that can never be loyal to the British crown, that its intellectual and moral values are at odds with modernity, that Islamic intellectual culture is essentially Greek, that Islam is irrational and mythic, then Iqbal retorts that Islam is a religion of peace, its intellectual culture is anti-classical, and it gave "birth to" inductive and scientific ways of interacting with empirical phenomena. *The Reconstruction* responds to the epistemic challenges of colonial modernity by generating a counter-polemic. Insofar as it perceives that its task is to offer binary claims that belie colonial depictions of the Qur'an, Muhammad, and Islam, it predicates features to Islam that contradict those that such scholarship attributes to it.

Style B, exemplified in Diagne, finds warrants in Iqbal's claims about how Islam's intellectual culture – and its history more broadly – embody plural and contradictory tendencies. It notes Iqbal's claims that a major problem in appreciating Islam is discovering how it reconciles permanence and change.[46] It finds telling examples where Iqbal describes *tawḥīd* (the oneness of God) as the synthetic activity of reconciling apparently contradictory predicates;[47] his insistence on dynamism and stasis as complementary processes at work in the history of Islamic thought;[48] and his suggestion of seeing Islam as processual, not as something that fully manifested itself at a point in history and is now passively reiterated by later generations of Muslims.[49]

Style C finds warrants where, as I argued above, *The Reconstruction* seeks to amend styles of predication that discredit the subject matter of their inquiry.[50] Javed Majeed, in similar vein, claims that Iqbal's volume challenges narratives and methods of inquiry that construct "Europe" and "Islam" in oppositional terms. Iqbal's strategies of "de-temporalizing" the history of thought and discussing thinkers such as Kant, Hegel, Rumi, and Darwin as if they were debating each other around a table disrupt forms of linear chronology that constrain conceptions only to the contexts of their production. *The Reconstruction* calls for rules of inquiry that conceive Islam as "in the making" and a "living force," rather than as fully formed, awaiting inquirers to unveil its character.[51] For Majeed, Iqbal seeks to articulate the "hitherto partially revealed purpose of Islam,"[52] a creative act that aims to enhance the rationality and significance of Islam and the Qur'an, not just observe and record them.

The three lines of inquiry discussed above present Iqbal's articulation of the "spirit of Islam" in different ways. Style A suggests that Iqbal sought consistency, stability, and permanence in the face of a polemically charged, chaotically progressive, and bewildering modernity; B, that he conceptualized Islam as a vague phenomenon; and C, that his primary concern was to transform methods of investigating Islam rather than securing a conception of what it is. As I have shown, *The Reconstruction* can support each of these three styles of reading, so applying only one will tend to over-generalize its conclusions beyond its domain of reference. For my purposes, Iqbal's practice of predicating features to Islam is a clear instance where the consequences of *The Reconstruction*'s representational and pragmatic voices are loudly at display. Style A displays Iqbal's representational voice, i.e., his tendency to conceptualize knowledge as binary, descriptive, as an unearthing of the "core" of the object of its analysis. B and C display the book's pragmatic tendencies. B reveals its willingness to admit certain objects of knowledge as vague. Any broad inquiry into Islam, B proposes, ought to employ conceptual apparatuses that allow an inquirer to attribute contradictory predicates to it. C exposes *The Reconstruction*'s tendency to make knowledge claims that require inquirers to correct their practices to address particular problems that ail their intellectual context.

In predicating features to Islam, *The Reconstruction*'s representational and pragmatic tendencies of knowing clash loudly. In discussing the spirit of Islam, Iqbal's text seems to haphazardly juggle polemics, apologetics, history, philosophical critique, and epistemological construction. His predicating of features to Islam reveals his pragmatic epistemic voice as he suggests that inquiries about Islam should look at the reception history of its founding discourses and employ tools that admit conceptual contradiction. He becomes representational when he conceptualizes Islam as the logical contradictory of colonial inquiries, arguing that true Islam opposes slavery, is peaceful, and is overlain with a Magian crust that needs to be discarded and a revolt against Greek intellectual culture.

My discussion now turns to the hermeneutical and epistemological patterns *The Reconstruction* employs as it discusses how the qur'anic text acquires meaning and referentiality. Just as this section discusses Iqbal's procedures for discovering Islam's meaning, the next outlines Iqbal's procedures for understanding the Qur'an.

II

Iqbal has described his literary output as intimately tied to the Qur'an.[53] He intended to write an explicative and introductory text on the Qur'an before his prolonged ailment and eventual death in 1938.[54] My purpose in this section is to selectively illustrate the representational and pragmatic elements in his practice of interpreting scriptural verses, as he productively links scripture, religion, and science.[55]

We can see Iqbal's representationalism most directly in his remarks on Q 24:35, or the light verse,[56] specifically the part that reads, "God is the Light of the heavens and the earth." He tells us that modern theories about the behaviour of light waves or photons undermine certain interpretations of the word light (*nūr*) and legitimize others: "The teaching of modern physics is that the velocity of light cannot be exceeded and is the same for all observers whatever their own system of movement. Thus, in the world of change, light is the nearest approach to the Absolute. The metaphor of light as applied to God, therefore, must, in view of modern knowledge, be taken to suggest the Absoluteness of God and not His Omnipresence."[57]

As Iqbal interprets this verse, he makes four significant epistemological moves:

- He interprets it as a descriptive proposition that corresponds to an object or state of affairs. This constitutes its primary function, as well as the route through which it acquires meaning. An interpretation of it is true insofar as it can faithfully *describe* what the verse is about.
- Iqbal assumes that other readers interpret the Qur'an and this verse in a manner identical to his own practice. Thus to qualify as a reader of this verse one has to assume the interpretive standpoint he has taken – attempting to describe accurately what the verse is about. So, for instance, Ḵẖvājah Mīr Dard, who reads it to mean

that God is omnipresent;[58] Ṭabarī, that God is a guide for all who inhabit the heavens and the earth;[59] Junayd, that God illuminates the hearts of angels, prophets, and believers;[60] and Ḥallāj, that it symbolizes God's oneness[61] – are all trying to figure out what this verse actually describes. In order to resolve which of these competing descriptions – God as omnipresent, as guide, as absolute, as one – is the accurate representation of the object of the verse, Iqbal turns to modern physics.

- Iqbal interprets modern physicists' activities in the same way as he did those of Qur'an readers. He describes the experimental activities of physicists in the form of a propositional claim, namely: "Light is the only absolute in the universe." Notice how this move is in tension with *The Reconstruction*'s claims about concepts employed by the various sciences. I showed in chapter 3 how Iqbal argued that physicists and biologists use concepts to regulate their expectations in relation to the phenomena they observe. In violation of his own cautions against hastily abstracting claims from the various sciences to deliver descriptions of reality, Iqbal takes physicists' claims about the velocity of light to describe given states of affairs.
- Lastly: The claim that "light is the only absolute in the universe" shows Iqbal that the verse "God is the Light of the heavens and the earth" represents the fact that "God is the only absolute in the universe." It also helps him to discard erroneous interpretations that read the verse as a description of God's omnipresence and so on.

Allied with the claims of relativity physics about light, Iqbal is able to identify the true referents of the qur'anic verse, whereas earlier exegetes, unaware of physics' new claims about light's behaviour, got it wrong when they read it as a description of God's omnipresence or God's function as a guide for all of creation.

This propositional procedure is also on display when Iqbal interprets part of Q 40:60 – "And your Lord has said: 'Call upon Me, and I shall respond to you'" – as a proposition identical with Josiah Royce's account of the reality of other minds.[62] Iqbal's hermeneutical manœuvres here resemble Sir Syed's procedure for making scientific and religious claims commensurable. The latter, as I showed in chapter 1, expands the semantic possibilities of the qur'anic text to offer a reading warrantable by the new sciences while being available to the Qur'an's original readers. For his representational side, Iqbal seems to have dropped Sir Syed's second criterion; Iqbal's reading seems available only to post-Einsteinian, contemporary readers. This difference only exacerbates the way Iqbal's representational take on the Qur'an (like Sir Syed's), as he tries to connect scriptural and scientific claims, involves him in an endless hermeneutics of war with other readers of the Qur'an.

The Reconstruction's pragmatic interpretation of scriptural claims is noticeable when Iqbal observes that the objects of qur'anic verses are displayed not generically, but with respect to context-specific interpretations of the text. He does this in two related styles, which I label forms I and II. When exemplifying form I, Iqbal notes that the verses of the Qur'an require their readers to *generate* certain habits in response to reading them, *which habits are the "objects" of those verses.* Form II is exemplified when Iqbal postulates that readers discover a verse's object not generically, but with respect to specific purposes and methods of reading.

Form I is clearest in Iqbal's reading of Q 49:6, specifically the part "O you who believe! If an iniquitous person comes to you with tidings, then be discerning." Iqbal claims that the activity of reading this verse led its readers to rethink what constitutes "trustworthiness." The verse does not correspond to a state of affairs, it demands and requires its readers to act a certain way in the world as a consequence of having read it. More specifically, Iqbal contends, it is one of the sources that inspired the creation of critical disciplines for analyzing Prophetic traditions.[63] Iqbal is not naïvely claiming that this verse contains clear directives for developing the science of hadith criticism. Instead, his claim is that reading this verse transforms its readers' lives and encourages them to generate such methods of inquiry. Form I implies that someone keen to investigate the Qur'an's meaning should conduct inquiries (historical, theological, lexical, ethnographic, and so on) into how *the text shapes and configures its readers' lives.* The multiple, evolving ways in which the Qur'an has done and continues to form and shape the lives of its readers constitutes the meaning of its verses.

Form II is clearest vis-à-vis Iqbal's reading of qur'anic verses that describe the movement or passage of "time" as a sign of God – for example, Q 10:6: "Surely in the variation of the night and the day and whatsoever God has created in the heavens and on the earth are signs for a people who are reverent." Iqbal's representational approach would have searched for sets of propositions that correspond to a state of affairs in the world as the meaning of such a verse. The claims of modern philosophy and science would have helped him accurately describe those states of affairs. Iqbal could, for example, say that a verse that states that "the alternation of the day and night is sign of God" describes the fact that "God is the source of life on earth," because modern ecology tells us that life would be impossible on earth but for the sun and the moon's consistent and recurrent behaviour in relation to the earth.

Instead, his comments suggest that he is sensitive to the notion that this verse's "meaning" is inextricably linked with and produced by various purposes and methods of engagement with it. Iqbal notes that for some mystical thinkers the words "the alternation of the day and night is a sign of God" establish practices of remembrance of God.[64] He hypothesizes that reading such verses is one factor that prompted some of them to "meditate" on the word "time" (*dahr*) as a way to establish intimacy with God.[65] For Ash'arite theologians, the verse guides their reasoning about the nature of time and its relationship with creation.[66] For a theological historian such as Ibn Khaldūn, such verses suggest the significance of "patterns" and "novelty" in the movement of history.[67]

Again, *The Reconstruction* is not arguing that this verse provides a clear blueprint for Ibn Khaldūn's account of history as a multi-layered dialectical movement. Instead, form II implies that someone interested in what a qur'anic verse means should look at how it guides and shapes its readers' inquiries and that the processes that one observes, and becomes implicated in, constitute its meaning.

Form II involves four key strategies for reading qur'anic verses:

- Iqbal assumes that verses' meanings display themselves through context and inquiry-specific engagement with them.
- In *The Reconstruction*, when Iqbal gives his own reading of verses about the alternation of night and day being a sign of God, he specifies his purpose. He seeks in part to resolve questions about characterizing God as "eternal." He wants to dispel the notion that predicating "eternity" to God makes time "unreal" in relation to God. He reads such verses as a resource for arguing that God's life, though eternal, contains within it elements of movement and alternation.[68]
- In looking to other readers of the same verses, Iqbal seeks to specify their contexts of inquiry and the purposes of their readings.
- Lastly: Iqbal does not see this multiplicity of inquiry and purpose-specific interpretations as necessitating conflict or opposition. Ibn Khaldūn, Iqbal, and other readers are not locked in an interminable conflict about these verses' true referents. Instead, a qur'anic verse can give rise to and participate in a variety of inquiries and purpose-specific processes of interpretation.

In brief, form I implies that someone inquiring into the meaning of purportedly revelatory texts should explore how such claims shape and configure their *readers' lives*. Their discoveries yield the practices, events, and phenomena that give those texts reference and meaning. Form II postulates that anyone investigating the "aboutness" of revelatory or scriptural claims should analyze how they shape their readers' *intellectual activities*.

Both forms make the new sciences and the scriptural resources of Islam commensurate by illustrating *The Reconstruction*'s general claim about religion: that religion names practices of inquiry concerned with a specific form of experience (i.e., *waḥī*), just as the various sciences interpret other forms of experience at the level of matter, life, and mind.[69]

I want to close this chapter by looking at how Iqbal's representational and pragmatic tendencies interact in his hermeneutical approach to the Qur'an. Throughout this book, I've proposed understanding the relationship between these two conceptions as "attempted repair." I'm going to outline the particular shape of this attempted repair vis-à-vis *The Reconstruction*'s scriptural hermeneutics in four steps. These are modifications and "cautions" that the pragmatic side of its scriptural hermeneutics makes to its representational counterpart:

- *The Reconstruction*'s pragmatic side cautions its representational side against taking qur'anic verses as non-contextual descriptions of the world. It urges linking referential claims, when offered as meanings of such verses, with the practices of inquiry out of which such claims emerge.
- It urges interpreters disagreeing with each other about the Qur'an's referential function to frame their claims not as descriptive propositions, but as inquiry and context-specific consequences of their reading of the Qur'an. In other words, warring readers should debate and share not just claims, but the methods or the investigative contexts of their claims, thereby making their differences more clear and precise.
- It suggests that differences of interpretation need not indicate or cause irreconcilable opposition, since interpreters are not producing mutually exclusive descriptions of a given state of affairs.
- Finally, it cautions against abstracting any individual claim from a given science and relating it to an abstracted claim about the "meaning" of a qur'anic verse. Instead, it seems to suggest that

> relationships between disciplines of inquiry such as physics, exegesis (*tafsīr*), and theology (*kalām*), if they are possible, are likely to emerge from examining and comparing their respective methods and patterns of inquiry and reasoning.

Are these pragmatic corrections discernible in Iqbal's own work? Certainly. Are the errors that these corrections are meant to heal also visible there? Quite so. How can a thinker enact both the problems they identify in others and ways to correct them? My contention, exemplified in this book, is that *criticism*, *correction*, and *repetition* of the problems thinkers identify in the world *mark* and *signal* their involvement in processes of repair.

CONCLUSION

Productive Tensions

My major task in this volume has been to diagnose and explicate the ambiguities and contradictions that permeate *The Reconstruction*'s project of articulating a rationality appropriate to religion, philosophy, and science.[1] In brief terms, my case has been that this philosophical project is beset by two distinct tendencies of what it means to know something. I have argued that *The Reconstruction*'s widely acknowledged, but misunderstood and under-theorized, equivocal, and confusing patterns of reasoning are traceable to the co-presence of its representationalist and pragmatic voices. I've traced how the book's representational voice (knowledge as descriptive, foundational, binary, and essential), for instance, characterizes its thematization of the "spirit of Muslim culture," part of its scriptural hermeneutics, and its use of *khudi* (selfhood) as a master category. I've simultaneously traced how *The Reconstruction*'s pragmatic voice (knowledge as performative, probabilistic, vague, and contextual) is audible, for instance, as Iqbal relates the categories of knowledge, experience, and reality; as he employs the category of selfhood to talk about human persons; as he criticizes scientistic approaches to philosophical and theological questions; and as part of the text's scriptural hermeneutics.

But why rehearse, in technical detail, the drama of the conceptions of knowing with which *The Reconstruction* wrestles? What is at stake in explicating and clarifying the epistemological tendencies that inform its theses about religion, philosophy, science, and their possible inter-relations? In this brief conclusion, I offer four comments on the possibilities that I imagine and hope my project may nourish for its readers.

First, this current volume addresses a major lacuna in the study of modern Islamic thought. Iqbal's *The Reconstruction of Religious Thought in Islam* has continuously and perennially been described as one of the most significant texts of modernist Islamic thought. Scholars have expertly situated Iqbal's thought in general, and *The Reconstruction* in particular, in the political, literary, sociological, and post-colonial contexts and prospects to which it is addressed. My project builds on and intervenes in such studies by paying sustained attention to the epistemological patterns and implications of *The Reconstruction*. On a related note, it also contributes to discussions in the young but growing field of "science and religion" by showing how a major text of modernist Islamic thought negotiates these categories.

Second, I hope to offer a hermeneutical approach to modern Islamic thought. Contemporary scholars have highlighted its aporias, tensions, and confusions by referring them to seismic shifts in the historical, political, and epistemological realities affecting modern Islamic thinkers. My work in this book complements this scholarship by studying how these crises are visible in the epistemological dynamics of philosophical thought generated in such moments of crisis. I have argued, through my reading of *The Reconstruction*, for looking at modern Islamic texts that perceive their intellectual contexts to be crisis-ridden and attempt to correct them as a dialogue between their own re-enactment of what they criticize and possible ways of redressing those crises. I have argued and performed a hermeneutical approach that reads texts of modern Islamic thought as embattled and wounded in their struggles to craft new ways for the Islamic intellectual tradition to bear truth and rationality in the context of modernity. My hermeneutical model – of reading such texts as tension-riddled dialogues that repeat and mend what they criticize – offers a non-reductive way of handling the complexity of such thought.

By displaying the intricacies of the way Iqbal's representational and pragmatic voices operate, I have not suggested that, ideally speaking, *The Reconstruction* would speak with one voice; that since Iqbal critiques representational epistemologies, he should speak only in a pragmatic vein. For a thinker who is utterly confounded by how young Muslims can be both modern and Muslim;[2] a public intellectual operating in a colonial environment that puts his very humanity into question,[3] it would be highly suspect if his thought did not bear the markings and wounds of his struggles.[4]

This kind of embattled and delegitimating epistemological and discursive context is evident in the letter exchanges surrounding Iqbal's invitation to give the Rhodes Memorial Lecture at Oxford University in 1934.[5] Iqbal responded positively and that he would like to speak on "Time and Space in the History of Muslim Thought." The secretary of the Rhodes Trust wrote back that the Rhodes lectures are of a public and "wider" nature than such a specialized topic and asked him to consider something of more general interest, such as "Islam in the Modern World." Iqbal agreed.

During these exchanges, the translator and novelist Edward Thompson, who was acting as a facilitator, wrote to the Trust's secretary that Iqbal was "very sensitive about the charge brought against Muhammadanism, that it is a sterile low-grade religion . . . giving nothing on the metaphysical side for the mind to bite on, infinitely inferior here to Christianity and Hinduism."[6] Iqbal is "ambitious, as his lectures show, to put Islam on the worldmap metaphysically . . . [and] wants to . . . prove that Islam has great philosophy and great philosophers."[7] Iqbal might mistakenly think that he has to "launch a world shaking philosophy" at Oxford, whereas his task, Thompson suggested, is "merely giving a jolly show for Islam."[8]

I have argued that the marks of *The Reconstruction*'s struggles against a delegitimating epistemic environment – where a thinker's philosophical work is received as "a jolly show for Islam" – are visible in the shape of the text's representationalist voice. *The Reconstruction*'s representational side is an indexical symptom of its involvement in a delegitimating context of inquiry. Its reiteration of the epistemological tendencies it seeks to transform is, if anything, an enabling condition; it is the most direct and easily identifiable locus to which the author's pragmatic side can speak. More broadly, I have argued that texts of modern Islamic thought – involved in intense epistemic conflicts about religion, philosophy, and science – are appropriately and rationally scarred and wounded by their participation in these epistemic battles.

My third comment is that *The Reconstruction*'s pragmatic side sketches a significant pattern for monitoring the excesses of representational ways of repairing a broken epistemic universe. For Muslim modernists, and others, who perceive their intellectual world as broken along lines such as religion and science, faith and reason, tradition and modernity, Iqbal's pragmatic voice sketches a useful pattern. It negotiates relation in difference while avoiding a notable error of representational ways of achieving coherence – namely, building relations within a conflicted domain of reference only by relocating that conflict to some other domain of reference. The clearest examples of this error that I have explored above are four in number: Sir Syed's construction of E_2, which sunders his exegetical practice from the exegetical tradition; Iqbal's discussion of the features of revelation (*waḥī*) that pits religious traditions against each other; Iqbal's predication of binary features to Islam that generates a counter-polemic against colonial scholarship; and Iqbal's representational scriptural hermeneutics, which places his interpretive claims at war with other readers. Iqbal's pragmatic side shows thinkers how to monitor potential excesses and over-generalizations when they try representational solutions.

And, lastly, the key thing at work in *The Reconstruction* is the way it *transforms* the representational facets of its epistemic environment into what I have called its pragmatic voice. The features I have isolated as *The Reconstruction*'s pragmatic voice, too, are potentially liable to the kinds of excesses that I have attributed to its representational voice. This sort of excess becomes possible, for instance, if its pragmatic voice is read as rejecting its representational inheritance, rather than transforming it. For example, it is possible to over-argue vagueness in situations that are more appropriately handled in binary terms. In the face of questions such as, "Is the salt shaker on the table or not?" a vague approach might be unhelpful. If an epistemic environment takes vagueness to reject appropriately binary claims, then it would likely repeat the errors it attributes to binary claims. I suppose I am sounding a cautionary note against a potential reading of my claims in this book. I am not suggesting that the pragmatic elements of Iqbal's thought simply generate a universe that is unproblematic because it is somehow protected from the kinds of excesses I have attributed to representational approaches. Neither am I suggesting imitating *The Reconstruction*'s pragmatic voice as a blueprint for gluing back together any and all broken or divided contexts of inquiry. Instead, in my reading, the interplay between representationalism and pragmatism in *The Reconstruction* suggests, to those of us whose universes are marked by crises analogous to the ones it addresses, to, in our own contexts, map logics of incorporating and transforming *our* epistemic inheritances. *The Reconstruction*'s re-enactment and transformation of its representational epistemic inheritance, then, creates a significant and productive site for observing the kinds of issues and complexities involved in attempting to address and transform a problematic epistemic environment.

Notes

INTRODUCTION

1 Ṣiddīqī, "Ah! Iqbāl."

2 For other, comparably eulogistic obituaries, see "Sir Muhammad Iqbal," 10; "Death of a Great Indian Muslim Poet"; "All-India Tributes."

3 Cf. Jansen, "Taḏjdīd"; Merad, Algar, Berkes, and Ahmad, "Iṣlāḥ."

4 Numerous biographies have been written on Iqbal. See, for instance: Javed Iqbal, *Zindah Rūd*; May, *Iqbal*; Shafique, *Iqbal: An Illustrated Biography.*

5 Iqbal Singh Sevea suggests that one of the ways to capture the range of Iqbal's activities is to think of him as an activist intellectual. See Sevea, *The Political Philosophy of Muhammad Iqbal*, 13.

6 Hassan, "Introduction," 1.

7 Ibid.

8 Smith, *Modern Islām in India.*

9 The purpose of the institution is "to promote and disseminate the study and understanding of the works and teachings of Allama Iqbal." For more, see http://www.iap.gov.pk/ <1 Jan. 2020>.

10 Apart from publishing books and hosting conferences and events that pertain to and curate Iqbal's legacy, the academy publishes English-, Persian-, and Urdu-language journals that focus on his life and work. For more, see http://allamaiqbal.com/publications/pub.htm <30 June 2020>.

11 Mir, *Iqbal*, 80. Several editions of *The Reconstruction* have been published over the years, commissioned by variously Oxford University Press, the Iqbal Academy Pakistan, and most recently Stanford University Press. All the citations from *The Reconstruction* in this text are from the Stanford edition (2012).

12 Suheyl Umar, former director of the Iqbal Academy Pakistan, and author of a commentary on *The Reconstruction*, suggests that its publication in English and

its complicated prose limited its readership in India (personal communication). See Umar, *Khuṭbāt-i Iqbāl*, 19–44.

13 Allen, "Signs of a Renaissance in Islam," 89.

14 Anwar, *The Epistemology of Iqbal*, 219. For other heroic assessments, see Abdul Razak, "Iqbal's Ideas for the Restoration of Muslim Dynamism"; Abdul Rahim, "The Spirit of Muslim Culture According to Muhammad Iqbal"; Whittemore, "Iqbal's Panentheism"; Ashraf, *A Critical Exposition of Iqbal's Philosophy*; Taylor, "Preface," xi–xii.

15 Margoliouth, Review of *The Reconstruction of Religious Thought in Islam*, 406.

16 Tritton, Review of *The Reconstruction of Religious Thought in Islam*, 694.

17 Maroof Shah, *Muslim Modernism and the Problem of Modern Science.*

18 This particular style of engaging *The Reconstruction* usually applies some philosophical criterion to its text and finds it lacking, or needing modification or a complete overhaul. See, for instance, Enver, *The Metaphysics of Iqbal*; Sharif, *About Iqbal and His Thought*; Saeeda Iqbal, "Muhammad Iqbāl's Dynamic Rationalism," 219–330; Haq, "Iqbal and Classical Muslim Thinkers." These three styles of criticism (heroic, dismissive, critical-constructive) name tendencies, and quite a few authors display more than one. For instance, Rahman, "Modern Muslim Thought."

19 I am thinking here of works such as Tareen, "Narratives of Emancipation in Modern Islam"; Majeed, *Muhammad Iqbal*, 116–34; Naveeda Khan, *Muslim Becoming*; Hillier, "Theo-Political Crisis and Reform"; Hillier, "Iqbal, Bergson and the Reconstruction of the Divine Nexus in Political Thought." Also see other essays in Hillier and Koshul, eds., *Muhammad Iqbal: Essays on the Reconstruction of Modern Muslim Thought*.

20 Hillier, "Theo-Political Crisis and Reform," 275–6.

21 Troll, *Sayyid Ahmad Khan*, 144–54. Also see Rizvi, "Between Hegel and Rumi."

22 Tayob, *Religion in Modern Islamic Discourse*, 33.

23 Majeed, "Introduction," xii.

24 Pickthall, *The Cultural Side of Islam*.

25 For an account of Iqbal's lecture tour, see Cug̱htā'ī, "'Allāmah Iqbāl Kā Janūbī Hind Kā Safar," 17–45, and Hāshimī, *Taṣānīf-i Iqbāl Kā Taḥqīqī o Tauẓīḥī Muṭāla'ah*, 313–23. Iqbal delivered the full six lectures only at Aligarh in November 1929. When he visited Madras and Hyderabad earlier that year, he presented just the three he had already finished. See Javed Iqbal, *Zindah Rūd*, 411–49.

26 Mir, *Iqbal*, 20.

27 Shafique, *Iqbāl: Daur-i 'Urūj*, 691.

28 Umar, *Khuṭbāt-i Iqbāl*, 176–81.

29 Pickthall, "Sir Muhammad Iqbal's Lectures."

30 Ibid., 678.

31 Ibid., 677.
32 Ibid., 683.
33 Ibid., 678.
34 Umar, *Khuṭbāt-i Iqbāl*, 10. Also see Iqbal, *The Reconstruction*, xlv–xlvii.
35 Iqbal, "The Muslim Community – A Sociological Study."
36 Iqbal uses variously the words "modernity," "the modern man," "modern thought and experience," "Europe," "the west" as synonyms throughout *The Reconstruction*.
37 Iqbal raises these concerns throughout the text, and I take them up in the following chapters.
38 Iqbal, "Presidential Address 1930," 6 (emphasis mine).
39 Cf. Rorty and Dewey's accounts of the western philosophical tradition: Rorty, *Philosophy and the Mirror of Nature*, and Dewey, *The Quest for Certainty*.
40 Cf. Reddy, "The Conduit Metaphor," 166–71.
41 George Lindbeck notes that a descriptive or propositional approach takes doctrinal claims to be "informative propositions . . . about objective realities . . . For a propositionalist, if a doctrine is once true, it is always true, and if it is once false, it is always false" (Lindbeck, *The Nature of Doctrine*, 2). Approaches that take religious doctrines to be descriptive claims about the world he terms "cognitivist."
42 Haack, "Descartes, Peirce and the Cognitive Community," 168.
43 Bernstein, *Beyond Objectivism and Relativism*, 8. Bernstein makes these remarks about what he labels "objectivism" – "closely related to foundationalism and the search for an Archimedean point" (ibid.).
44 Ochs, "Re-socializing Scholars of Religious, Theological, and Theo-philosophical Inquiry," 208–9.
45 In Ochs's more technical terms: "The binarist assumes, for example, that some term (X) names a given object in the world (O), that some clear proposition involving X (X is Y) is true because it corresponds directly to some claim about O (O is Y), and that any apparently contradictory claim about O (O is Z) contradicts the true proposition and is therefore false" (ibid., 209).
46 See Adams's account of Hegel's reception of western philosophy and his attempt to redress its shortcomings in *Eclipse of Grace*, 1–16.
47 Tayob, *Religion in Modern Islamic Discourse*, 23–48.
48 I explore these claims in detail in the following chapters.
49 Cf. Collingwood's reflections on the "logic of question and answer" in Collingwood, *An Autobiography*, 29–43.
50 Faizi, "Why Saying 'Only Some Muslims Are Violent' Is No Better Than Saying 'All Muslims Are Violent,'" 85.
51 Cf. Lindbeck, *The Nature of Doctrine*, where he argues that a performative approach to religious claims analyses how such claims shape, constitute, and are

employed in the lives of the people who utter them. Lindbeck also notes that performative claims involve propositions or descriptions. The way I handle the function of propositions in performative claims is an issue I clarify below in this chapter. Similarly, Andrew Pickering, in *The Mangle of Practice*, distinguishes representational and performative "idioms" of expressing scientific knowledge generation: a representational idiom "casts science as, above all, an activity that seeks to represent nature, to produce knowledge that maps, mirrors, or corresponds to how the world really is" (5), while a performative approach imagines the world filled "with *agency* … continually *doing things* . . . Much of everyday life . . . has [the] character of coping with material agency . . . My suggestion is that we should see science . . . as a continuation and extension of this business of coping with material agency" (6–7).

52 What I'm calling knowledge as performative here is close to Dewey's conception of knowledge as an instrument of inquiry. See Dewey, *Logic* and *The Quest for Certainty*.

53 Cf. Cattelan, "Alice's Adventures, Abductive Reasoning and the Logic of Islamic Law." Cattelan notes that Islamic jurisprudential reasoning functions according to a "probabilistic logic." Also see Ochs's discussion of "regressive reasoning" in Ochs, "Reparative Reasoning."

54 Cf. Peirce, *Collected Papers of Charles Sanders Peirce*, ed. Hartshorne and Weiss (hereafter CP), vol. 5, para. 505.

55 Kang, "Mapping Triadic Vistas."

56 Ibid.

57 Weiss, *Paradox and the Prophets*, 34. Weiss notes that "if certain ideas or practices resist theoretically consistent descriptions, how does this change our criteria for a 'rational account' of a given subject? It may be that a text's rationality is better measured by its ability to *avoid* one-sidedness than by its 'autonomous' theoretical coherence" (ibid.).

58 Shahab Ahmed, *What Is Islam?*, 405–541.

59 Cf. Adams, "Long-term Disagreement," 162–3. What Adams notes about "gesturing towards" one's environment in making a claim about an object is similar to how Seuren describes the role of "discourse" in discourse-oriented conceptions of language. See Seuren, *Western Linguistics*, 400–5. Also see CP, vol. 2, paras. 233–53

60 All these claims are explored in detail in the following chapters.

61 Peirce's classic description of what the word "lithium" refers to is particularly instructive here: "If you look into a textbook of chemistry for a definition of *lithium*, you may be told that it is that element whose atomic weight is 7 very nearly. But if the author has a more logical mind he will tell you that if you search among minerals that are vitreous, translucent, grey or white, very hard,

brittle, and insoluble, for one which imparts a crimson tinge to an unluminous flame, this mineral being triturated with lime or witherite rats-bane, and then fused, can be partly dissolved in muriatic acid; and if this solution be evaporated, and the residue be extracted with sulphuric acid, and duly purified, it can be converted by ordinary methods into a chloride, which being obtained in the solid state, fused, and electrolyzed with half a dozen powerful cells, will yield a globule of a pinkish silvery metal that will float on gasolene; and the material of *that* is a specimen of lithium. The peculiarity of this definition – or rather this precept that is more serviceable than a definition – is that it tells you what the word lithium denotes by *prescribing what you are to do in order* to gain a perceptual acquaintance with the object of the word" (CP, vol. 2, para. 330) (emphasis mine). The key thing here is that the description of lithium involves propositions that prescribe precepts or rules of action, rather than seeking to mirror the reality of lithium. Cf. Stjernfelt, *Natural Propositions*.

62 In his analyses of the appropriate domain of reference of binary claims, Ochs writes: "'Binarism' is a strong tendency to overstate and over-generalize the usefulness of either/or distinctions. I assume that we appropriately rely on such distinctions whenever we seek to communicate something clearly: when, for example, someone says 'pass the salt,' meaning 'salt and not pepper.' But I also assume that such communications are appropriate only within groups of language users who tend to share common understandings of some sets of terms and only in settings where communication does not require ambiguity or judgments of probability. 'Binarism' refers only to the inappropriate application of either-or distinctions to settings of irremediable ambiguity and probability" (Ochs, "Re-socializing Scholars of Religious, Theological, and Theo-philosophical Inquiry," 208–9).

63 Deely, *New Beginnings*, 151–82.

64 These essays have been collected in a sixteen-volume collection of Sir Syed's extensive essays, pamphlets, and articles: Aḥmad, Khan *Maqālāt-i Sar Sayyid*. For a detailed biography of Sir Syed, see Ḥālī, *Ḥayāt-i Jāvīd*.

65 Cf. Pink, "Striving for a New Exegesis of the Qur'ān"; Wielandt, "Exegesis of the Qur'ān"; Ahmad, *Islamic Modernism in India and Pakistan*, 31–56.

66 Tayob, *Religion in Modern Islamic Discourse*, 32.

67 Dar, *Letters of Iqbal*, 153.

68 Hassan, "Introduction," 1. For Hassan's dissertation on Iqbal, see Hassan, "The Main Philosophical Idea in the Writings of Muhammad Iqbal." For her philosophical review and assessment of Iqbal's corpus, see Hassan, *An Iqbal Primer*.

69 Majeed, *Muhammad Iqbal*, 123–8.

70 Additionally, by identifying Iqbal as a modernist and juxtaposing him against another, I do not mean to rehearse the facile binary between traditionalist

reformers and modernists. Iqbal's political writings, his poetry, and his prose have a foot in all the camps of nineteenth- and twentieth-century reformist thought that Sajjad Rizvi identifies in South Asian intellectual history. Each of these "camps" or "tendencies" produced its own sets of "modernisms" because of its location within the apparatus of colonial modernity. See Rizvi, "Between Hegel and Rumi," 112–13.

71 Cf. Umar, *Dar-i Ā'īnah Bāz Hai*, 59–61.

72 Transliterated variously as *k̲h̲udī*, *k̲h̲ūdī*, and *k̲h̲vudī* in sources. Since some sources, including Iqbal's letters, have used "*khudi*," without transliteration, I follow this convenient convention.

73 Suheyl Umar lays out such questions in detail in *Dar-i Ā'īnah Bāz Hai*, 57–67.

74 Haq, "Iqbal and Classical Muslim Thinkers."

75 Cf. Umar, *Dar-i Ā'īnah Bāz Hai*, 64, and Făzli, "Iqbal's View of Omniscience and Human Freedom," 141, 145.

76 Faruqi, "How to Read Iqbal?" and "Is Iqbal, the Poet, Relevant to Us Today?"

77 I am not suggesting that my theses about the epistemological dimensions of *The Reconstruction* may not apply to other elements of Iqbal's work and life. Exploring this question may be one way to test the generalizability of my work on *The Reconstruction* to other aspects of Iqbal's work. I'm trying not to place *The Reconstruction* precisely within his extensive corpus but to display its epistemic dynamics.

78 This is why, within *The Reconstruction*, too, I have focused on and elaborated themes that are most pertinent to Iqbal's theses about religion, philosophy, and science.

79 See how the concept "value" is used in Ochs et al., "Value Predicate Analysis."

CHAPTER ONE

1 Sir Syed Ahmed Khan's name has been anglicized and transliterated in numerous ways in the secondary literature. I've picked the anglicized Sir Syed Ahmed Khan for the main body of this work. For bibliographical referencing, I've consistently transliterated his name as Sayyid Aḥmad K̲h̲ān. Readers will find all works attributed to him under the transliterated version of his name in the bibliography.

2 See Dar, "Sayyid Ahmad and Modernism," and Dar, *Religious Thought of Sayyid Ahmad Khan*. For a recent account of Sir Syed's modernism as a critique of colonial discourses, see Hussain, "Islam as Critique." For an account and illustration of the way Sir Syed shaped modernist concerns in India, see al-Rahim, "Translation as Contemporary Qur'anic Exegesis."

3 Aḥmad K̲h̲ān, "Qur'ān Majīd Kī Tafsīr Ke Uṣūl."

4 See Rahbar, "Sir Sayyid Aḥmad Ḵẖān's Principles of Exegesis." Rahbar notes: "Sir Sayyid's Commentary is in fact a collection of essays and not a word by word *Tafsīr*. He comments only on his limited selection of verses relating to the questions which he considered most important for his times" (ibid., 105). The text of *Taḥrīr Fī Uṣūl al-Tafsīr* I cite in this chapter is from Aḥmad Ḵẖān, "Qur'ān Majīd Kī Tafsīr Ke Uṣūl."

5 For his biography see Zubairī, *Ḥayāt-i Muḥsin*. Also see Khan, "A Great Stalwart of the Aligarh Movement."

6 Sir Syed's ancestral home was ransacked during this conflict, and by all accounts, including his own, it was a shattering ordeal for him. After the *g̱hadr* (rebellion) he wrote copiously to dispel the notion that it was a "Muslim" uprising, arguing that Muslims could be fully Muslim and fully loyal to the crown. For more, see Aḥmad Ḵẖān, *An Account of the Loyal Mahomedans of India*; Aḥmad Ḵẖān, *The Causes of the Indian Revolt*; Graham, *The Life and Work of Sir Syed Ahmed Khan*, 15–48; Hasan, *A Moral Reckoning*, 8–18.

7 Aḥmad Ḵẖān, "Qur'ān Majīd Kī Tafsīr Ke Uṣūl" 198.

8 See Baljon, *The Reforms and Religious Ideas of Sir Sayyid Ahmad Khan*, 43–58; Graham, *The Life and Work of Sir Syed Ahmed Khan*, 49–63.

9 Aḥmad Ḵẖān, "Qur'ān Majīd Kī Tafsīr Ke Uṣūl," 198–9.

10 Ibid., 200.

11 Mehdi Ali clarifies these particular objections in his second letter to Sir Syed. See Ibid., 218–9. For an introductory account on the place of angels and the *jinn* in Islamic intellectual history, see MacDonald et al., "D̲j̲inn"; MacDonald and Madelung, "Malā'ika."

12 Aḥmad Ḵẖān, "Qur'ān Majīd Kī Tafsīr Ke Uṣūl" 201–2. Mehdi Ali closes his letter with the following request: "Nothing would please me more than you relieving me of my doubts. Because in many places [your exegesis] is so noble (*'umdah*) and pure (*pākīzah*) and elevated (*a'lá*) that, after the Qur'an and hadith, if someone were to recite it and learn it by heart, he would [gain the status] of a scholar (*'ālim*) and true Muslim in this world and would be deserving of the rewards that God has reserved for true Muslims in the world to come" (ibid., 202).

13 Ibid., 201.

14 Ibid., 202.

15 Sir Syed tells Mehdi Ali: "You may think my work wrong, you may not accept it but [neither your upbringing nor your trust in the *'ulamā* and *mufassirīn*] is grounds for claiming that my work is contrary to God's purposes" (ibid., 204).

16 Ibid., 207.

17 Ibid., 209.

18 Ibid.

19 Ibid., 212–14. Mehdi Ali continues: "Hence a great European thinker in a popular book – where he denies God's power and intentionality and knowledge . . . has described God only as a necessary first cause . . . He says '[that belief in a necessary first cause rather than a personal God] is free of old ideas and more reasonable than them. Doubtless, it requires its adherents to be strong of heart [in comparison with weak-willed religious believers].' . . . And another one of them says: 'That which people call a creator God is, in fact, a creation of people themselves and a personification of human attributes.' . . . He thinks people who believe in God are fools and idiots . . . and he says about a pure book like the Gospel (*Injīl*) that, 'in my opinion, in order for any intelligent person to be convinced that the Gospel is a human creation, and a barbaric one at that, all they have to do is give it a read . . . rid your eyes of the blindfold of devotion, your heart of fear, and your mind of spurious thoughts . . . [and you shall blame yourself] for considering, even for a minute . . . that the author of this work is rational, and good, and pure.' These are not the ideas of one or two authors but most of those familiar with science look upon religious people . . . with bewilderment and pity. Unless one reaches that pinnacle of knowledge wherefrom these people [speak] one appears to them as entrapped by ancestral ideas [about God, Prophets, resurrection, and salvation]" (ibid., 214–15).

20 Ibid., 220–1.

21 Ibid., 220.

22 Ibid., 222.

23 Ibid.

24 Sir Syed's conception of nature and its relationship with scripture forms his central principle of exegesis of the Qur'an. I take up this conception in the following paragraphs.

25 See Kang, "Mapping Triadic Vistas."

26 Aḥmad Ḵẖān, "'Ulūm-i Jadīdah."

27 Aḥmad Ḵẖān, "Taraqqī-yi 'Ulūm," 215.

28 I show in the next paragraph that Sir Syed imagines not only that knowledge is akin to a building but that the object of one's knowledge is also like a building. In fact, an inquirer must, to the best of their capacity, identify the foundations for the object of knowledge and then construct the house of knowledge on identical foundations.

29 In Haack's terms ("Descartes, Peirce, and the Cognitive Community"), Sir Syed imagines that the knowledge claims of a particular epoch (*zamānah*) are based on a set of epistemologically privileged and (seemingly) incorrigible and self-legitimating assumptions.

30 Aḥmad Ḵẖān, "Qur'ān Majīd Kī Tafsīr Ke Uṣūl," 200.

31 Ibid., 239.

32 Ibid., 206. Cf. ibid., 246.

33 Ibid., 239–40.

34 Ibid., 246.

35 Ibid.

36 Ibid., 206.

37 Aḥmad Ḵẖān, "Mu'jizah Kī Ḥaqīqat," 84.

38 Aḥmad Ḵẖān, "Qur'ān Majīd Kī Tafsīr Ke Uṣūl," 206.

39 Aḥmad Ḵẖān, "Mu'jizah Kī Ḥaqīqat," 79.

40 Troll, "Sir Sayyid Ahmad Khan, 1817–98, and His Theological Critics," 326. Ali Bakhsh was an adversary of Sir Syed's, who acquired various fatwas from India as well as from Mecca denouncing and anathematizing his approach to the Qur'an. According to Ḥālī, Sir Syed's biographer and associate, these fatwas declare Sir Syed to be the representative (*ḵẖalīfah*) of the Devil himself who is intent upon leading Muslims astray. See Ḥālī, *Ḥayāt-i Jāvīd*, vol. 2, 184.

41 Troll, *Sayyid Ahmad Khan*, 175.

42 Metcalf, *Islamic Revival in British India*, 323.

43 Reetz, "Enlightenment and Islam," 215. Peter Byrne marks out two elemental features of deism. First, religion is not tied to any specific historical moment and is beyond culture and history. Second, God's interaction with creation is uniform, law-bound, and universal. For Byrne's general overview of deistic conceptions of God, see Byrne, *Natural Religion and the Nature of Religion*, 52–78.

44 The title of this essay translated in English reads: "Does Naturalism Mean that God Is Absolved?" See Aḥmad Ḵẖān, "Kyā Necar Ke Mānne Se Ḵẖudā Mu'aṭṭal Ho Jātā Hai?"

45 Ibid., 283.

46 Ibid., 283–4

47 Ibid., 285.

48 Sir Syed's conception of human agency in relation to the course of nature proceeds according to more usual deistic lines. Since everything in the universe occurs according to a set measure (*muqaddar*), the subjective wishes and prayers of prophets and ordinary human beings do not have any bearing on the occurrence of events in nature. Admitting the efficacy of petitionary prayer would amount to admitting that miraculous events that contravene nature do occur. It would also introduce a veiled form of anthropomorphism in the events of nature since they would be directly subject to the wishes and desires of human beings. In more concrete terms, God cannot be petitioned to (miraculously) cure diseases, bring about rain, or influence the results of the lottery. However, this does not mean that the activity of prayer can be abandoned altogether. Prayer is an "instinctive" (*fiṭrī*) act and can significantly alter the subjectivity of one who prays. It grants one the patience (*ṣabr*) and fortitude

(*istiqlāl*) required to bear the burdens of life. The "objective" consequences of prayer are displayed in its transformation of the attitude and activities of one who prays, not in any fantastic, supernatural occurrences. See Aḥmad Ḵẖān, "Du'ā Aur Uskī Qubūliyat."

49 This should not be taken to mean that Sir Syed imagines that the character of these patterns is mechanistic and Newtonian and that his formal commitment advances either a physicalist or a reductively mechanistic picture of creation. See Aḥmad Ḵẖān, "Mu'jizah Kī Ḥaqīqat," 78–91.

50 Ibid., 84.

51 Ibid.

52 Ibid., 82. Also see Aḥmad Ḵẖān, "Qur'ān Majīd Kī Tafsīr Ke Uṣūl," 230–8, and Troll, *Sayyid Ahmad Khan*, 176.

53 Aḥmad Ḵẖān, "Qur'ān Majīd Kī Tafsīr Ke Uṣūl," 207.

54 Sir Syed comments: "The meanings that I attribute to the speech of God and the speech of the Prophet, I firmly believe that God and God's Prophet have spoken those words to convey the meanings I attribute to them" (Aḥmad Ḵẖān, "Sar Sayyid Kā Aṣl Maẓmūn," 139).

55 Aḥmad Ḵẖān, "Qur'ān Majīd Kī Tafsīr Ke Uṣūl," 254–7. My work in the second section of this chapter illustrates my claims about the function and purpose of Sir Syed's hermeneutical principles.

56 Ibid., 256.

57 Ibid., 254.

58 Aḥmad Ḵẖān, "Qur'ān Majīd Kī Tafsīr Ke Uṣūl," 240–1.

59 This is a modified translation from Ahmad and Grunebaum, *Muslim Self-Statement in India and Pakistan 1857–1968*, 38–9. For the original, see Aḥmad Ḵẖān, "Qur'ān Majīd Kī Tafsīr Ke Uṣūl," 255–7.

60 Modified from Ahmad and Grunebaum, *Muslim Self-Statement in India and Pakistan 1857–1968*, 39. For the original, see Aḥmad Ḵẖān, "Qur'ān Majīd Kī Tafsīr Ke Uṣūl," 256.

61 Troll, *Sayyid Ahmad Khan*, 147.

62 Aḥmad Ḵẖān, "Qur'ān Majīd Kī Tafsīr Ke Uṣūl," 257.

63 Ibid.

64 The examples from Sir Syed's exegesis that I discuss in the next section illustrate this point.

65 As I mentioned above, the case in relation to the Qur'an is slightly more complicated: the progress of the exegetical tradition consists in discovering or recovering elements of the Qur'an's original reception and God's intentions with respect to that reception.

66 Aḥmad Ḵẖān, "Jinnon̲ Kī Ḥaqīqat," 152.

67 Modified translation from Ahmad and Grunebaum, *Muslim Self-Statement in India and Pakistan 1857–1968*, 36. For the original, see Aḥmad Ḵẖān, "Qur'ān Majīd Kī Tafsīr Ke Uṣūl," 249–50.

68 Aḥmad Ḵẖān, "Jibrā'īl o Mīkā'īl Aur Farishtoṉ Kā Vujūd," 164–5.

69 For Sir Syed's applications of this hermeneutic device, see Aḥmad Ḵẖān, "Farishtoṉ Aur Shaiṯān Kī Ḥaqīqat," "Ḥaẓrat 'Īsá Kī Paidā'ish Aur Vafāt Kā Mas'alah," "Ḥaẓrat 'Īsá Ke Mu'jizāt," and "Jibrā'īl o Mīkā'īl Aur Farishtoṉ Kā Vujūd."

70 Aḥmad Ḵẖān, "Jinnoṉ Kī Ḥaqīqat," 152.

71 Sir Syed laments that Muslim exegetes in their analyses of the Qur'an have uncritically taken up such fantastic and unreal ideas of pre-Islamic Arabs as the intended and real meaning of the Qur'an's usage of the word "*jinn*." See Aḥmad Ḵẖān, "Jinnoṉ Kī Ḥaqīqat"

72 Ibid., 155.

73 Sir Syed's interpretive scheme for reading the *jinn* mentioned in *sūrah jinn* is unique to it. He states that it was a habitual practice of the disbelievers in Mecca to furtively listen to the Prophet of God. *Sūrah jinn* is a narrative account of one of these occurrences wherein the Prophet's recital of the Qur'an was overheard by Meccans who were "concealed" from his sight. The "*jinn*" in the *sūrah* refers to these concealed individuals, who converted to Islam because of the powerful influence of Muhammad's recitation. Sir Syed argues that several verses of the *sūrah* corroborate his interpretation of the *jinn* as human beings, since these verses indicate that the *jinn* held Christian, Jewish, and polytheistic beliefs. See Aḥmad Ḵẖān, "Sūrah Jinn Kī Tafsīr," 137–43.

74 Aḥmad Ḵẖān, "Ḥaẓrat 'Īsá Ke Mu'jizāt," 362.

75 Ibid., 362–6.

76 Ibid., 366.

77 Ibid.

78 Aḥmad Ḵẖān, "Mūsá, Fir'aun Aur Banī Isrā'īl," 170–8.

79 Ibid., 158.

80 Ibid. 158–9.

81 In one of his essays, Sir Syed writes about witnessing mesmerism during public events in Benares that included brief lectures on the practice as well as practical demonstrations. The professor would mesmerize volunteers from the audience and make them perform various odd deeds. For more, see Aḥmad Ḵẖān, "Mismirīzam." For an account of the development and applications of the science contemporary to Sir Syed, see Esdaile, *Mesmerism in India and Its Practical Application in Surgery and Medicine*. For the complicated practice of mesmerism within colonial medicine, see Ernst, "Colonial Psychiatry, Magic and Religion."

82 In "Mismirīzam," Sir Syed explicitly links mesmerism with "'*ilm al-Sīmiyā*'." See Aḥmad Khān, "Mismirīzam," 288. For an introduction to the various connotations and meanings of the term, see MacDonald and Fahd, "Sīmiyā."

83 These are the terms in which Mehdi Ali describes Sir Syed's task in the correspondence I recounted above in this chapter. Mehdi Ali notes: "Please do not think that I am unaware of the need that compelled you to write your exegesis or that I am unaware of the cacophonous war between religion and science being waged in our time. Or that I think that the attack that knowledge, in a new form, with newly forged weapons, is carrying out against religion is minor. Or that I think our existing books are sufficient [for responding to the attacks of science] ... Probably very few people would be more desirous than me that religion ought to be protected against the attack of science ... [I recognize that] you have entered this war against science with a white flag and have tried to make peace with such an over-powering and great foe" (Aḥmad Khān, "Qur'ān Majīd Kī Tafsīr Ke Uṣūl," 217).

84 Ochs, *Another Reformation*, 6–7.

85 Cf. ibid. I've simplified Ochs's model. Here are his own words:

- collecting examples of an offending practice (a, b, c ... n);
- suggesting that this collection displays a class character that can be defined according to a finite set of propositions, or, in other words, reduced to a relatively simple propositional function [P = (a, b, c ... n), where P = f (x)];
- promoting another practice (Q) as both the desirable alternative to the offending practice (P) and the desirable means of repairing P (or of repairing institutions that errantly pursue P);
- assuming that Q can also be defined according to a finite set of propositions (which therefore corresponds to another relatively simple propositional function [Q = (x, y, z ... n), where Q = g (x)]);
- intentionally or unintentionally, therefore, presupposing that Q and P are logical contradictories – in other words, that both P and Q refer to a domain of possible practices (W), such that the domain is served by either P or Q (W = P∪Q), where P ≠ Q (Ochs, *Another Reformation*, 6–7).

He continues: "This is a mode of reparative argument that generates comparable sets of antagonistic postures regardless of the goal of one's argument. It makes secularists, religionists, rationalists, and irrationalists all partners to exclusivist and dogmatic politics and positivist epistemologies. They are positivist because Q is knowable by way of sets of clear and distinct propositions; they are exclusivist because Q ≠ P, which means we know that practices will be either Q or P, that Q is correct and that it excludes P" (ibid., 7).

CHAPTER TWO

1 Iqbal, "New Year Message," 298.
2 Cf. Tareen, "Narratives of Emancipation in Modern Islam."
3 Iqbal, "New Year Message," 298.
4 Iqbal, "Presidential Address 1932," 31.
5 Devji, "Illiberal Islam," 238. Devji expresses Iqbal's ethico-political and epistemic critique of modernity: "[For Iqbal] territorial belonging brought into being the dominance of property over all the relations of social life, such that all interests became interests of ownership. Indeed the nation-state could even be characterized by a mode of knowledge for which the world was composed entirely of things that had to be grasped proprietorially . . . Representation, then, whether epistemological or political, was the very model of discursive reason because it grasped both persons and objects as forms of property, to be weighed, counted, and worshipped not only in the practices of democracy, but also in those of knowledge as such . . . As far as the liberal order of the nation state was concerned, its unhappiness for Iqbal was made possible by the metaphysical division of society into public and private realms, with the ideal, the spiritual . . . being confined to a private life in which it could function only as ineffective moralism and mere ideal" (ibid., 239).
6 Iqbal, "Presidential Address 1930," 3–10; Iqbal, "Presidential Address 1932," 30–2.
7 Iqbal, "Presidential Address 1930," 6.
8 Iqbal, *The Reconstruction*, 132.
9 Ibid.
10 Ibid.
11 Umar, *Khuṭbāt-i Iqbāl*, 10.
12 As readers discover in the next section, *The Reconstruction* does not describe these terms clearly at one place in the text. The first section of this chapter analyzes how these terms function in *The Reconstruction* by inspecting their various appearances in the text.
13 Ibid., 1. Chapter 1 of *The Reconstruction* begins with a volley of questions: "What is the character and general structure of the universe in which we live? Is there a permanent element in the constitution of this universe? How are we related to it? What place do we occupy in it, and what is the kind of conduct that befits the place we occupy? These questions are common to religion, philosophy, and higher poetry" (ibid.).
14 Iqbal, *Tashkīl-i Jadīd Ilāhiyāt-i Islāmiyah* (the title of Niazi's translation of Iqbal's *Reconstruction*).
15 Niazi, "Muqaddamah," 7–10.
16 Iqbal, *Tashkīl-i Jadīd Ilāhiyāt-i Islāmiyah*, 291.

17 Iqbal, *The Reconstruction*, 10.

18 Ibid., 86.

19 Ibid., xlv.

20 Ibid., 10.

21 Ibid., 15.

22 Ibid., 21.

23 Ibid., 156.

24 Ibid., 62.

25 Ibid., 10–11.

26 Ibid., 15.

27 Ibid., 10.

28 Ibid., 33.

29 Ibid., 10–12, 86, 156–7.

30 I say "agent" here because *The Reconstruction* employs the concept of knowledge not just for individual consciousness, after the fashion of the ego-cogito, but also for activities of, for example, bees, plants, as well as human communities. Ibid., 3, 100.

31 Ibid., 12.

32 Ibid.

33 Ibid., 14.

34 Ibid., 13.

35 Ibid.

36 Ibid., 18.

37 Ibid., 20.

38 Ibid., 14.

39 Ibid., 12.

40 Ibid., 147.

41 Ibid., 10.

42 Ibid., 15.

43 Ibid., 13.

44 Ibid., 90.

45 Ibid., 14

46 Ibid., 13

47 We see in the third section of this chapter that *The Reconstruction* violates its three-part contextual conception of knowledge.

48 *CP*, vol. 2, paras. 227–308.

49 Morris, "Foundations of the Theory of Signs."

50 Petrilli and Ponzio, *Semiotics Unbounded*.

51 Nöth, *Handbook of Semiotics*.

52 Deely, *Basics of Semiotics*.

53 Yelle, “Semiotics.”

54 Cf. Sebeok, *A Sign Is Just a Sign*, 13, 83; Deely, “Semiotics ‘Today,’” 48, 92, *passim*; CP, vol. 3, paras. 456–78.

55 This simplified model of semiotic analysis is adequate for our present purposes. For more involved distinctions between elements of semiosis and numerous other models, see Morris, “Foundations of the Theory of Signs”; Nöth, *Handbook of Semiotics*; CP, vol. 2, paras. 243–331; Sebeok, *Signs*.

56 Smith, *What Is Scripture?*

57 Ibid., 1–21.

58 Iqbal, *The Reconstruction*, 41

59 Iqbal, “Self in the Light of Relativity,” 110–11.

60 Iqbal, *The Reconstruction*, 30–1

61 Cf. Deely, “From Semiosis to Semioethics.” For Deely’s technical treatment of the distinctions I just named, see his *New Beginnings* and *The Impact on Philosophy of Semiotics*.

62 Iqbal, *The Reconstruction*, 13.

63 Ibid., 20, 99.

64 Ibid., 20.

65 Ibid., 1–22 *passim*.

66 Ibid., 2–3.

67 Ibid., 20.

68 Ibid., 144.

69 Ibid., 149–50.

70 Ibid., 86.

71 Ibid., 33–4, 144–5.

72 Ibid., 34.

73 Ibid., 143–57.

74 Ibid., 20.

75 Ibid., 13.

76 Ibid., chapter 2 *passim*.

77 Ibid., 15.

78 Ibid., 20.

79 Ibid., 151.

80 Ibid., 18.

81 Quoted in Rizvi, “Between Hegel and Rumi,” 117.

82 Iqbal, *The Reconstruction*, 26.

83 All this is consistent with the notion that the term “experience” functions as a sign-vehicle, mediating knowledge and reality; its “features” or “character” displays itself with respect to some form of investigation.

84 Iqbal, *The Reconstruction*, 20.

85 Ibid., 26
86 Ibid., 20.
87 Ibid., 156.
88 Ibid., 144.
89 Ibid., 156.
90 Ibid., 155.
91 Ibid., 14.
92 Ibid.
93 Ibid.
94 Ibid., 15.
95 Ibid.
96 Ibid.
97 Ibid (emphasis mine).
98 Ibid.
99 Ibid., 16
100 Ibid., 18.
101 This is a particularly vexing debate in Islamic theology. Cf. Van Ess, "Verbal Inspiration?"; Griffel, "Muslim Philosophers' Rationalist Explanation of Muḥammad's Prophecy"; Michot, "Revelation."
102 Iqbal, *The Reconstruction*, 18.
103 Ibid.
104 Cf. Sharif, *About Iqbal and His Thought*, and Enver, *The Metaphysics of Iqbal.*
105 See Schimmel, *Gabriel's Wing*, 316–76.
106 Javed Iqbal, *Zindah Rūd*, 86–7.
107 Iqbal, *The Reconstruction*, 162.
108 Cf. Adams, "Iqbal and the Western Philosophers." Adams makes this case in relation to Iqbal's use of western philosophy, but it is a more general feature of *The Reconstruction*, especially vis-à-vis mystical experience.
109 Iqbal, *The Reconstruction*, 143.
110 Ibid., 145.
111 Ibid., 34.
112 Ibid., 143.
113 Ibid., 12, 155.
114 According to Khurram Ali Shafique (personal communication), Iqbal's most prolific intellectual historian and biographer, three essays (two lectures, one publication) by Iqbal are important base-texts of *The Reconstruction* as well as his philosophical thought more broadly: "Islam as a Moral and Political Ideal," "The Muslim Community – A Sociological Study," and "Political Thought in Islam."
115 Iqbal, "Islam as a Moral and Political Ideal," 97–117.
116 Ibid., 98–102.

117 Ibid., 101.

118 Ibid.

119 Ibid.

120 Ibid.

121 Ibid., 102. Iqbal's more detailed rendition of these propositions is as follows: "(1) There is pain in nature and man regarded as an individual is evil (Buddhism). (2) There is sin in nature and the taint of sin is fatal to man (Christianity). (3) There is struggle in nature; man is a mixture of struggling forces and is free to range himself on the side of the powers of good which will eventually prevail (Zoroastrianism)" (ibid., 101).

122 Ibid., 117.

123 Iqbal, *The Reconstruction*, 114.

124 This is a constant refrain throughout ibid., perhaps exemplified most fully in chapter 5, 99–115.

125 Ibid., 7–8.

126 Iqbal, "Islam as a Moral and Political Ideal," 102.

127 Iqbal, *The Reconstruction*, 122.

128 Ibid., 124. Iqbal attributes these views to Said Halim Pasha and, echoing his agreement, observes that they are "in tune with the spirit of Islam" (Ibid.). Also see Schimmel, *Gabriel's Wing*, 242–4.

129 Iqbal, "Statement on Islam and Nationalism," 302–3. This is an English translation of a newspaper article published in Urdu. For the original, see Iqbal, "Jug͟hrāfiyā'ī Ḥudūd Aur Musalmān."

CHAPTER THREE

1 For Arberry's translation, see Iqbal, *Mysteries of Selflessness.*

2 See Iqbal, *Kullīyāt-i Iqbāl.*

3 The construction in Urdu is pointedly paradoxical.

4 Shafique, *Iqbāl: Darmiyānī Daur*, 127.

5 Iqbal, *Secrets of the Self*, xvii.

6 Mir, *Iqbal*, 31.

7 Ibid.

8 Majeed, *Muhammad Iqbal.*

9 See, for instance, Diagne, "Achieving Humanity."

10 Rafiuddin, "Iqbal's Idea of the Self."

11 Houben, "The Individual in Democracy and Iqbal's Conception of Khudi."

12 Bausani, "Iqbal."

13 Ahmad, "Sources of Iqbal's Idea of the Perfect Man."

14 Hassan, "Iqbal's 'Khudi.'"

15 Malik, "Iqbal's Conception of Ego."

16 Wheeler, "Individual and Action in the Thought of Iqbal."

17 Shahab Ahmed, *What Is Islam?*, 329–30.

18 Ibid., 340. "Questions about whether and how a person can access the Truth of Revelation . . . about the authority of human reason as a means of knowing . . . about the validity of (altered states of) human consciousness as a means of knowing (i.e., debates over Sufism), about the constitution of human agency and responsibility (debates over predestination and freewill, or *qaḍā'* and *qadar*), are all ultimately questions about the nature and constitution and experience and capacity of the individual Self relative to the Truth of Revelation . . . The Muslim predicament of hermeneutical engagement with Revelation is directly productive of a trajectory of Self-interrogation, Self-contemplation, Self-affirmation, Self-articulation, and Self-action as means to meaning in terms of Islam" (ibid., 330).

19 Ibid., 329–31 *passim*. Ahmed notes that disciplines as wide-ranging as mysticism (taṣawwuf), theology (*kalām*), and philosophy (*falsafah*) have elaborated and reflected on selfhood as they have explored revelation and its relationship with Muhammad, God, God's creation, and historically variegated Muslim communities.

20 Ibid., 340. Ahmed adds: "Iqbāl . . . effectively sought to make of every Muslim a *muḥaqqiq*/self-realizer of Truth" (ibid.).

21 Cf. Koshul, "Muhammad Iqbal's Reconstruction of the Philosophical Argument for the Existence of God." Iqbal's use of the concept of *khudi* in *The Reconstruction* is a prime example of how a philosophical "master category" functions.

22 Iqbal, *The Reconstruction*, 33.

23 Ahmed, *What Is Islam?*, 363–7, 430–5.

24 Cf. Iqbal, *The Reconstruction*, xlv, and "Islam as a Moral and Political Ideal," 107–10.

25 Iqbal, "The Muslim Community – A Sociological Study," 130–1.

26 Ibid.

27 Iqbal, *The Reconstruction*, 21.

28 Ibid.

29 Ibid. (emphasis mine).

30 This is the heading of chapter 2 of *The Reconstruction*: "The Philosophical Test of the Revelations of Religious Experience."

31 M. Saeed Sheikh suggests that one of Iqbal's purposes in *The Reconstruction* is to show that "It is not logically impossible to be a great Muslim as well as a great scientist and philosopher" (Sheikh, "Iqbal as a Modern Interpreter of Islam," 77).

32 Iqbal, *The Reconstruction*, 25–6. The full verse reads, "He [God] is the First (*al-Awwal*), and the Last (*al-Ākhir*), and the Outward (*al-Ẓāhir*), and the Inward (*al-Bāṭin*); and He is Knower of all things."

33 Iqbal, *The Reconstruction*, 26.

34 Ibid.

35 Ibid., 23–5.

36 Ibid., 28.

37 Ibid., 26.

38 Ibid.

39 In Iqbal's words, this bifurcation "between Nature and the observer of Nature . . . creates a gulf . . . [which is then bridged] over by resorting to the doubtful hypothesis of an imperceptible something, occupying an absolute space like a thing in a receptacle and causing our sensation by some kind of impact" (ibid., 27).

40 Ibid., 27–8, 86, 147.

41 Ibid., 33.

42 Ibid., 34.

43 Ibid., 33.

44 Ibid., 28.

45 Ibid.

46 Iqbal, "Self in the Light of Relativity," 111.

47 Iqbal, *The Reconstruction*, 28.

48 Ibid., 31.

49 Ibid., 33.

50 Ibid., 33–4.

51 Ibid. 33.

52 Ibid., 34.

53 Ibid., 34–5.

54 Ibid., 36.

55 For a comprehensive historical survey of debates that were raging between emergentists in the wake of Darwin and later, see Blitz, *Emergent Evolution*. For contemporary debates about the applicability of "emergence" as an analytical framework, see Corning, "The Re-emergence of Emergence, and the Causal Role of Synergy in Emergent Evolution."

56 Iqbal, *The Reconstruction*, 33–6.

57 Ibid., 34.

58 Ibid., 85.

59 Ibid.

60 Ibid., 37.
61 Readers may recall that Iqbal abandons his contextual employment of knowledge, experience, and reality in relation to some of his arguments about religion and revelation as well.
62 Iqbal, *The Reconstruction*, 37.
63 Ibid. (emphasis mine).
64 Ibid.
65 Ibid., 38.
66 Ibid., 38–43.
67 Ibid., 44.
68 Ibid., 49.
69 Ibid.
70 Ibid., 48–9 (emphasis mine).
71 Ibid., 21.
72 Ibid., 25–6.
73 Ibid., 45.
74 For a broad sense of the various receptions of Iqbal's theological work, see Noorani, "Muhammad Iqbal and the Immanence of God in Islamic Modernism."
75 Sharif, *About Iqbal and His Thought*, 4.
76 Ibid., 6.
77 Ibid., 26
78 Ibid., 26–30. Sharif writes: "Both [Iqbal and Ward] hold on exactly the same grounds and in exactly the same sense that God is an infinite, conscious, omnipotent and omniscient spirit, which is immanent in the finite egos and yet transcends them . . . For both He is a perfectly free creative spirit that limits its own freedom by creating free finite egos, and for both this internal limitation is not inconsistent with His own perfect freedom" (ibid., 28).
79 Majeed, "Putting God in His Place," 230.
80 Ibid., 210.
81 Noorani, "Muhammad Iqbal and the Immanence of God in Islamic Modernism," 63–4.
82 Raschid, *Iqbal's Concept of God*, xvii.
83 Ibid., xv.
84 Ibid., xvii
85 Whittemore, "Iqbal's Panentheism," 698. Noorani notes that Whittemore is one of the first scholars to have attributed the label of "panenetheism" to Iqbal's work (Noorani, "Muhammad Iqbal and the Immanence of God in Islamic Modernism," 63).

86 Ibid., 694. Hartshorne and Reese include Iqbal as a "modern panentheist" in their broad anthology of philosophical conceptions of God. See Hartshorne and Reese, *Philosophers Speak of God*, 294–7.

87 Whittemore, "Iqbal's Panentheism," 699.

88 Nguyen, *Modern Muslim Theology*, 9.

89 Koshul, "Muhammad Iqbal's Reconstruction of the Philosophical Argument for the Existence of God," 99.

90 Farhan Shah, "Towards a Process-Humanistic Interpretation of Islam," 96.

91 Noorani, "Muhammad Iqbal and the Immanence of God in Islamic Modernism," 65.

92 Ibid. For Noorani, Iqbal's "conception of God as an immanent, order-generating principle . . . finds its material realization through the evolution of the universe, and more specifically, through the activity of the collective agent that embodies this principle in history and brings about an ultimate union of the spiritual and the material. Iqbal's God, therefore, in an important sense, is not a pre-existing entity, but a potentiality within the universe that can only come fully into being through human effort. This notion enabled Iqbal to depict individuals as self-ordering, creative agents who give rise to a Muslim 'nation'" (ibid., 61). Noorani also observes: "Examining the issues raised by the nature and role of God in Iqbal's metaphysical vision allows us to isolate a key element in Islamic modernist thought – the need to identify an immanent, organizing principle of human history that finds its full expression in an Islamic social order, and the tension that thereby arises with traditional Islamic notions of God" (ibid., 60). The basic "effect of Iqbal's theory of divinity is the type of historical framework it can motivate and the type of community it can posit. It is able to make Islam the key element of an ideal nationhood and the axis of a developmental world history" (ibid., 67).

93 Sheikh, "Iqbal as a Modern Interpreter of Islam," 78.

94 Iqbal, *The Reconstruction*, 49.

95 Ibid., 57.

96 Ibid.

CHAPTER FOUR

1 Iqbal, *The Reconstruction*, 57.

2 Forster, "The Poetry of Iqbal," 804.

3 Dar, *Letters of Iqbal*, 141.

4 Ibid.

5 Ibid.

6 Cf. Shabab Ahmed, *What Is Islam?*, 79. The perfect or complete human, or *al-Insān al-Kāmil*, is a complex and integral issue in the anthropological reflections of thinkers such as Ibn al-ʿArabī, Azīz-i Nasafī, and ʿAbd al-Karīm al-Jīlī (see ibid.). Cf. Arnaldez, "al-Insān al-Kāmil"; Knysh, *Ibn ʿArabi in the Later Islamic Tradition*; Little, "al-Insān al-Kāmil"; Chittick, "The Perfect Man as the Prototype of the Self in the Sufism of Jāmī." For Iqbal's essay on al-Jīlī, see Iqbal, "The Doctrine of Absolute Unity as Expounded by Abdul Karim al-Jilani."

7 Dar, *Letters of Iqbal*, 146.

8 Ibid., 142–3. The quote Iqbal adduces is originally from Mackenzie, *An Introduction to Social Philosophy*, 438–40.

9 Dar, *Letters of Iqbal*, 147.

10 Schimmel, "Man of Light or Superman?," 136.

11 Ibid., 138. Schimmel notes "Faustian" themes in Iqbal's conception of human personhood as well.

12 Ahmad, "Sources of Iqbal's Idea of the Perfect Man," 17. Ahmad adds that "at other times [Iqbal's Perfect Man] is *Momin*, the Perfect Man who has passed the three stages of Jili's mystic training . . . Occasionally there is a glimpse of the Mephistophelian Superman in an individual whom Iqbal tries to recondition and rehabilitate; but this is rare" (ibid.).

13 Ibid., 17.

14 Azad, "Reconstructing the Muslim Self," 15.

15 See https://www.punjab.gov.pk/information_and_culture_institutions <15 Oct. 2020>.

16 Sharif, "Editorial," i.

17 Rafiuddin, "Iqbal's Idea of the Self." Rafiuddin continues passionately, "[This world state shall bring] to man all the blessings of permanent peace and unity and [enable] him to achieve that highest progress – material, mental, moral and spiritual of which the promise resides in the potentialities of their nature" (ibid.).

18 Schimmel, *Gabriel's Wing*, 74. According to Schimmel, the "task for Iqbal, and his fellow-reformers, was to come to a re-interpretation of the traditional symbols, so that the outworn forms were filled again with life" (ibid.).

19 Ibid., 382.

20 Ibid., 111.

21 Moosa, "The Human Person in Iqbal's Thought," 13.

22 Ibid., 29.

23 McDonough, "Iqbal," 403–13. McDonough comments: "Human purposes develop, in Iqbal's opinion, in inter-action with the one God who is best understood by the metaphor of a self-conscious self – the Ultimate Ego. The English expression 'I-Thou' relationship best characterises this insight; the opposite is an

'I-it' relationship in which the human is a person but everything else has the status of object to be manipulated according to the needs and wishes of the human person" (ibid., 409).

24 Ibid., 409.

25 Ibid.

26 Cf. Ochs, "Iqbal, Peirce and Modernity."

27 Naveeda Khan, *Muslim Becoming*, 76.

28 Various strands (theological, political, genealogical) of reflection on Iqbal's notion of *khudi* may be expressed and clarified in the same work. See, for instance, ibid.; Majeed, *Muhammad Iqbal*; Shahab Ahmed, *What Is Islam?*

29 Sevea, *The Political Philosophy of Muhammad Iqbal*, 29.

30 Ibid.

31 Ibid., 139–44.

32 Noorani, "Islamic Modernity and the Desiring Self," 123.

33 Ibid.

34 Ibid., 133.

35 Ibid.

36 Ibid. Noorani writes that, for Iqbal, "The modernity of the West is a historical wrong turn, an inauthentic form of relating to the world akin to the decadence of the classical *ghazal*. The empiricist, calculative approach of Enlightenment rationality is an attempt to possess and accumulate the objects of the world rather than to transform them into the self. It is therefore yet another form of enslavement to the world of everyday time. It leads not to the utopian political order promised by Islam but to the exploitation and tyranny of capitalism and colonialism. Similarly, the political legacy of the classical *ghazal* and its absorption in the beauty of the external world is the voluntary enslavement to the false and transient pleasures of Western domination. Just as the *ghazal* poet gleefully succumbs to the tyranny of the beloved, so do modern Muslims happily deliver themselves to European rule . . . On this basis Iqbal depicts the colonial situation not simply as a struggle between Islam and Western Imperialism but as a moral and historical drama of the self" (ibid., 133).

37 Majeed, *Muhammad Iqbal*, 23. According to Majeed, this is one of two contexts that mark Iqbal's concept of selfhood, the other being "notions of selfhood in circulation in Islamic artistic and philosophical culture" (ibid., 20). For Majeed's rendition of this context see ibid., 20–2.

38 Shahab Ahmed, *What Is Islam?*, 340.

39 Ibid., 341.

40 As mentioned above, Iqbal uses the words "soul," "ego," and "person" synonymously in *The Reconstruction*.

41 Ibid., 85.

42 Iqbal asks, provocatively, "Are then the soul and its organism, two things in the sense of Descartes, independent of each other, though somehow mysteriously united?" (ibid., 83).
43 Ibid., 83–5.
44 Ibid., 84.
45 Ibid., 86 (emphasis mine).
46 Ibid., 94.
47 Ibid., 85.
48 Ibid., 94.
49 Adams elaborates this vocabulary in his logical studies of how Hegel constructs relations between concepts such as being–non-being and self–other. See Adams, *Eclipse of Grace.*
50 Ibid., 9.
51 Ibid.
52 Ibid.
53 Smith, *What Is Scripture?*, 17–18.
54 Sevea, *The Political Philosophy of Muhammad Iqbal*, 110. Sevea notes: "The two key works in which Iqbal discussed his views on the development of the individual and society are his *Asrar-i-Khudi* and *Rumuz-i-Bekhudi*. Conventionally, these texts are studied as separate literary works. The emphasis on the *khudi* . . . in his *Asrar-i-Khudi* has led to the work being described as a [poem] which sought to provide the modernist message of the free development of the individual. The *Rumuz-i-Bekhudi*, on the other hand, is widely characterised as a work which sought to curb the threat of excessive individualism. Contrary to such views, the ideas expressed in the two works are not distinct. Iqbal's personal letters and notes reveal that [they] were not written as separate poems but rather were conceived of as parts of the same [poetical work] . . . In order to gain a comprehensive insight into Iqbal's views on the individual and society, it is imperative to approach the ideas developed in [the two works] as expressions of the whole of his ideas" (ibid., 140-1).
55 Iqbal, *The Reconstruction*, 80.
56 Dar, *Letters of Iqbal*, 153.
57 Iqbal, *The Reconstruction*, 78.
58 Moosa, "The Human Person in Iqbal's Thought," 12–13.
59 Ibid., 14.
60 Iqbal, *The Reconstruction*, 80–2.
61 Ibid., 80.
62 Adams, *Habermas and Theology*, 32.
63 Iqbal, *The Reconstruction*, 80–5.

64 Cf. Deely, *Medieval Philosophy Redefined*; Kevelson, "Transfer, Transaction, Asymmetry," 7–8; *CP*, vol. 1, paras. 239–41. Iqbal's procedure is akin to what these philosophers identify as cenoscopy but is not identical with it.

65 Readers will have noticed that arguments that count as cenoscopic in a room full of physicists will be very different from those that so qualify in a room hosting anthropologists.

66 Iqbal, *The Reconstruction*, 86 (emphasis mine). Iqbal also observes that "the element of guidance and directive control in the ego's activity clearly shows that the ego is a free personal causality" (ibid.). His reliance on cenoscopic evidence is also fully on display when he's persuading *The Reconstruction*'s audience that human personhood is characterized by "privacy." He notes that when one goes to the dentist, the dentist "may sympathize with my toothache, but cannot experience the feeling of my toothache. My pleasures, pains, and desires are exclusively mine, forming a part and parcel of my private ego alone" (ibid., 80).

67 Ibid., 87.

68 Several philosophers, including Kant, Dewey, and Peirce, have developed analytical vocabularies appropriate to phenomena that are exemplified in and guide or shape a given practice. Cf. Kant on regulative ideals, Dewey on habits, and Peirce on what he calls "thirds."

69 Iqbal, *The Reconstruction*, 87.

70 Naveeda Khan, *Muslim Becoming*, 55–90; Shahab Ahmed, *What Is Islam?*, *passim*.

71 Naveeda Khan, *Muslim Becoming*, 175.

72 Sevea, *The Political Philosophy of Muhammad Iqbal*, 109.

73 Iqbal, *The Reconstruction*, 97.

74 Ibid.

75 Ibid., 95.

76 Ibid., 98.

77 Ibid., 95.

78 Ibid., 96.

79 McClure, "Reconstructing Islam in a Post-metaphysical Age," 143.

CHAPTER FIVE

1 Iqbal, *The Reconstruction*, 48.

2 Ibid., 44.

3 My analysis in this section is analogous to how I explored Iqbal's predication of features to human *khudi* in chapter 4, and it is readable as an analysis of how Iqbal predicates features to the *khudi*, or self, of Islam.

4 Ibid., 100.

5 M. Saeed Sheikh, *The Reconstruction*'s editor, clarifies Iqbal's interpretation of *waḥī* in the Qur'an: "Though *wahy matluww* (revelation which is recited or worded revelation) is specific to the Prophets, the Qur'an speaks of revelation in connection with earth (99:5), heavens (41:12), honey-bee (16:68–69), angels (8:12), mother of Moses (28:7) and disciples of Jesus (5:111)" (Iqbal, *The Reconstruction*, 184).

6 See Iqbal, "Islam as a Moral and Political Ideal," 107–10, and "The Muslim Community – A Sociological Study," 130–3.

7 Mir, *Iqbal*, 2–3; Javed Iqbal, *Zindah Rūd*, 82–5; Shafique, *Iqbal*, 16.

8 Javed Iqbal, *Zindah Rūd*, 142–3.

9 Ibid., 143.

10 Ibid.

11 MacDonald, *The Religious Attitude and Life in Islam*, 45–6.

12 Margoliouth, *Mohammed and the Rise of Islam*, 45–6.

13 Nicholson, *A Literary History of the Arabs*, 147–8.

14 Iqbal, *The Reconstruction*, 150.

15 MacDonald, *The Religious Attitude and Life in Islam*, 46.

16 Iqbal, *The Reconstruction*, 99.

17 Ibid.

18 Burney, *Kulliyat Makateeb-e-Iqbal*, vol. 3, 119.

19 Iqbal, *The Reconstruction*, 99.

20 Iqbal's analyses here strongly complement the way Robert Orsi describes the consequences of overly determined sociological and psychological analyses of religious experience. Orsi says, "Many (not all) scholars of religion become restive sooner or later with the simple sufficiency of explanations of religious phenomena and experiences in terms of the social and psychological . . . They recognize that such accounts fall short of the realness of the phenomena they purport to describe and explain in people's experience. And not just this: social accounts that pretend to be exhaustive distort those experiences and diminish them, *precisely as* historical and cultural phenomena . . . The famous epistemic 'bracket' of religious studies . . . we are not interested in whether or not the Blessed Mother *really* appeared to Bernadette at Lourdes, we say, thus immediately making the seer into a psychotic – begins to seem false or inadequate" (Orsi, "The Problem of the Holy," 84–5).

21 Tayob, *Religion in Modern Islamic Discourse*, 46.

22 Ibid., 44. Tayob notes that the "extra-historical" core of Islam that Iqbal posits is in the service of the creation of "dynamic" individuals who act as "agents of history" (ibid., 35).

23 Ibid., 47, 35.

24 Tayob comments that the stable and permanent predicates that Iqbal and other modernists sought to attribute to Islam were conceptualized by them as visible and operative throughout Islam's history and became available through Muhammad's revelatory experience.

25 Diagne, *Islam and Open Society*, 54–5, *passim*.

26 Shahab Ahmed, *What Is Islam?*, 405–541.

27 Diagne, *Islam and Open Society*, 51–4.

28 Majeed, *Muhammad Iqbal*, 116–33.

29 Iqbal, *The Reconstruction*, 100.

30 Ibid., 104.

31 Ibid., 101.

32 Ibid.

33 Ibid.

34 Ibid.

35 Ibid., 102–14

36 These claims are sprinkled throughout the text of *The Reconstruction* and presented most systematically in chapter 5.

37 Ibid., 104–5.

38 See Dewey, *Reconstruction in Philosophy*.

39 Iqbal, *The Reconstruction*, 105.

40 Ibid., 2–3.

41 Ibid., 104.

42 Ibid., 103–4

43 Iqbal, "Islam as a Moral and Political Ideal," 106. Iqbal states that the "truth is that the institution of slavery is a mere name in Islam" (ibid.).

44 Ibid., 111.

45 Ibid., 114.

46 Iqbal, *The Reconstruction*, 117.

47 Ibid.

48 Ibid., 132.

49 Ibid., 113, 132, 134, 142.

50 See my arguments at the beginning of this section about how *The Reconstruction* urges focus on the consequences rather than the genesis of the purportedly revelatory as a more useful way to predicate features to Islam, Muhammad, and the Qur'an.

51 Majeed, *Muhammad Iqbal*, 120–2.

52 Iqbal, *The Reconstruction*, 142.

53 Afzaal, "Iqbal's Approach to the Qur'an," 13.

54 Schimmel, *Gabriel's Wing*, 223.

55 Schimmel offers a vivid picture of Iqbal's relationship with the Qur'an in ibid., 220–51.

56 This verse has generated endless reflection throughout Islamic intellectual history; for a sampling, see Böwering, "The Light Verse."

57 Iqbal, *The Reconstruction*, 51.

58 Schimmel, *Gabriel's Wing*, 100. According to Schimmel, Dard reads the metaphor of light in the Qur'an to refer to God's omnipresence and absolutism.

59 Nasr, *The Study Quran*, 878.

60 Böwering, "The Light Verse," 133.

61 Ibid., 134–5.

62 Iqbal, *The Reconstruction*, 15–16.

63 Ibid., 111–12. See Scarcia Amoretti, "ʿIlm al-Ridjāl."

64 Iqbal, *The Reconstruction*, 58–9.

65 Ibid.

66 Ibid., 59.

67 Ibid., 112–13.

68 Ibid., 58–62.

69 See chapter 3 above, "Knowledge, Experience, and Reality." The implications of forms I and II and styles B and C resemble Shahab Ahmed's recent proposals for conceptualizing Islam. In *What Is Islam?*, Ahmed writes: "Conceptualizing Islam as meaning-making for the Self in terms of Pre-text, Text, and Con-Text of Revelation cultivates in us the cognitive and analytical habit of looking for Islam in discursive and paraxial diffusion: in the full range of thought and action by which Muslims engage with sources of Revelation and with the Con-Textual language of its meanings. It enables us to detect and recognize Islam not just in the usual places where our received cognitive and analytical habits lead us, but where it actually is present in discourse and praxis as means and meanings . . . To do otherwise is to impoverish and distort the *meaning* of those acts and statements – which are rendered less meaningful than they actually are precisely in the measure that it is Islam, the hermeneutical engagement, which gives them meaning – and is, thus, to impoverish and distort the meaning of Islam" (544–5).

CONCLUSION

1 More technically:

- I have collected the set (X) of *The Reconstruction*'s theses about relationships between religion, philosophy, and science.

- I have found and trusted secondary scholarship that has observed confusion in *The Reconstruction*'s theses about those relations.
- I hypothesize that this confusion flows from the operation of the book's two epistemological tendencies – representational and pragmatic.
- Thence I hypothesize further that the set of claims (X) is isolatable into two subsets (X_1, X_2), each defined by a consistent epistemological tendency, neither of them confusing.

2 Iqbal, "The Muslim Community – A Sociological Study," 118–37.

3 Recall the missionaries with whom Iqbal spent an evening in Scotland.

4 It could perhaps even challenge his claims about his crisis-ridden context.

5 Ḥusain, *'Allāmah Muḥammad Iqbāl.*

6 Ibid., 28.

7 Ibid.

8 Ibid. About the correspondence between Iqbal and Thompson, see S. Hasan Ahmad, *Iqbal, His Political Ideas at Crossroads.*

Bibliography

Abdul Rahim, Adibah. "The Spirit of Muslim Culture According to Muhammad Iqbal." *International Journal of Social Science and Humanity* 5, no. 8 (2015): 725–9.

Abdul Razak, Mohd Abbas. "Iqbal's Ideas for the Restoration of Muslim Dynamism." *Journal of Islam in Asia* 8, no. 2 (2011): 377–402.

Adams, Nicholas. *Eclipse of Grace: Divine and Human Action in Hegel*. Hoboken, NJ: Wiley-Blackwell, 2013.

– *Habermas and Theology*. Cambridge: Cambridge University Press, 2006.

– "Iqbal and the Western Philosophers." In *Muhammad Iqbal: A Contemporary*, ed. Muhammad Suheyl Umar and Basit Bilal Koshul, 69–77. Lahore: Iqbal Academy Pakistan, 2010.

– "Long-Term Disagreement: Philosophical Models in Scriptural Reasoning and Receptive Ecumenism." *Modern Theology* 29, no. 4 (2013): 154–71.

Afzaal, Ahmed. "Iqbal's Approach to the Qur'an." In *Muhammad Iqbal: A Contemporary*, ed. Muhammad Suheyl Umar and Basit Bilal Koshul, 7–26. Lahore: Iqbal Academy Pakistan, 2010.

Ahmad, Aziz. *Islamic Modernism in India and Pakistan: 1857–1964*. London: Oxford University Press, 1967.

– "Sources of Iqbal's Idea of the Perfect Man." *Iqbal: A Journal of the Bazm-i Iqbal* 7, no. 1 (1958): 1–17.

Ahmad, Aziz, and G.E. Von Grunebaum, eds. *Muslim Self-Statement in India and Pakistan 1857–1968*. Reprint. Lahore: Suhail Academy, 2004.

Ahmad, S. Hasan. *Iqbal, His Political Ideas at Crossroads: A Commentary on Unpublished Letters to Professor Thompson, with Photographic Reproductions of the Original Letters*. Aligarh: Printwell Publications, 1979.

Aḥmad Kẖān, Sayyid (Sir Syed). *An Account of the Loyal Mahomedans of India*. 2 vols. Meerut: Mofussilite Press, 1860.

– *The Causes of the Indian Revolt*. First pub. in Urdu 1859. Benares: Medical Hall Press, 1873.

– "Du'ā Aur Uskī Qubūliyat." In *Maqālāt-i Sar Sayyid*, ed. Muḥammad Ismā'īl Pānīpatī, 2nd ed., vol. 13, 55–64. Lahore: Majlis-i Taraqqī-yi Adab, 1993.

– "Farishtoṉ Aur Shaiṭān Kī Ḥaqīqat." In *Maqālāt-i Sar Sayyid*, ed. Muḥammad Ismā'īl Pānīpatī, 2nd ed., vol. 13, 177–85. Lahore: Majlis-i Taraqqī-yi Adab, 1993.

– "Ḥaẓrat 'Īsá Ke Mu'jizāt." In *Maqālāt-i Sar Sayyid*, ed. Muḥammad Ismā'īl Pānīpatī, vol. 14, 348–73. Lahore: Majlis-i Taraqqī-yi Adab, 1965.

– "Ḥaẓrat 'Īsá Kī Paidā'ish Aur Vafāt Kā Mas'alah." In *Maqālāt-i Sar Sayyid*, ed. Muḥammad Ismā'īl Pānīpatī, vol. 14, 310–47. Lahore: Majlis-i Taraqqī-yi Adab, 1965.

– "Jibrā'īl o Mīkā'īl Aur Farishtoṉ Kā Vujūd." In *Maqālāt-i Sar Sayyid*, ed. Muḥammad Ismā'īl Pānīpatī, 2nd ed., vol. 13, 157–76. Lahore: Majlis-i Taraqqī-yi Adab, 1993.

– "Jinnoṉ Kī Ḥaqīqat." In *Maqālāt-i Sar Sayyid*, ed. Muḥammad Ismā'īl Pānīpatī, vol. 2, 150–96. Lahore: Majlis-i Taraqqī-yi Adab, 1961.

– "Kyā Necar Ke Mānne Se Ḵẖudā Mu'aṭṭal Ho Jātā Hai?" In *Maqālāt-i Sar Sayyid*, ed. Muḥammad Ismā'īl Pānīpatī, 2nd ed., vol. 3, 283–5. Lahore: Majlis-i Taraqqī-yi Adab, 1984.

– "Mismirīzam." In *Maqālāt-i Sar Sayyid*, ed. Muḥammad Ismā'īl Pānīpatī, 2nd ed., vol. 4, 288–99. Lahore: Majlis-i Taraqqī-yi Adab, 1988.

– "Mu'jizah Kī Ḥaqīqat." In *Maqālāt-i Sar Sayyid*, ed. Muḥammad Ismā'īl Pānīpatī, 2nd ed., vol. 13, 78–91. Lahore: Majlis-i Taraqqī-yi Adab, 1993.

– "Mūsá, Fir'aun Aur Banī Isrā'īl." In *Maqālāt-i Sar Sayyid*, ed. Muḥammad Ismā'īl Pānīpatī, vol. 14, 153–225. Lahore: Majlis-i Taraqqī-yi Adab, 1965.

– "Qur'ān Majīd Kī Tafsīr Ke Uṣūl." In *Maqālāt-i Sar Sayyid*, ed. Muḥammad Ismā'īl Pānīpatī, vol. 2, 197–258. Lahore: Majlis-i Taraqqī-yi Adab, 1961.

– "Sar Sayyid Kā Aṣl Maẓmūn." In *Maqālāt-i Sar Sayyid*, ed. Muḥammad Ismā'īl Pānīpatī, 2nd ed., vol. 3, 112–75. Lahore: Majlis-i Taraqqī-yi Adab, 1984.

– "Sūrah Jinn Kī Tafsīr." In *Maqālāt-i Sar Sayyid*, ed. Muḥammad Ismā'īl Pānīpatī, vol. 2, 137–49. Lahore: Majlis-i Taraqqī-yi Adab, 1961.

– "Taraqqī-yi 'Ulūm." In *Maqālāt-i Sar Sayyid*, ed. Muḥammad Ismā'īl Pānīpatī, 2nd ed., vol. 7, 213–15. Lahore: Majlis-i Taraqqī-yi Adab, 1991.

– "'Ulūm-i Jadīdah." In *Maqālāt-i Sar Sayyid*, ed. Muḥammad Ismā'īl Pānīpatī, 2nd ed., vol. 7, 211–12. Lahore: Majlis-i Taraqqī-yi Adab, 1991.

Ahmed, Shahab. *What Is Islam? The Importance of Being Islamic*. Princeton, NJ, and Oxford: Princeton University Press, 2016.

"All India Tributes." *Times of India*, 22 April 1938.

Allen, Henry E. "Signs of a Renaissance in Islam." *Journal of Religion* 15, no. 1 (1935): 88–90.

al-Rahim, Ahmed H. "Translation as Contemporary Qur'anic Exegesis: Ahmed Ali and Muslim Modernism in South Asia." In *The Two-Sided Canvas: Perspectives on Ahmed Ali*, ed. Mehr Afshan Farooqi, 136–50. New Delhi: Oxford University Press, 2013.

Anwar, Khurshid. *The Epistemology of Iqbal*. Lahore: Iqbal Academy Pakistan, 1996.

Arnaldez, R. "al-Insān al-Kāmil." In *Encyclopaedia of Islam: Second Edition*, ed. P. Bearman, Th. Bianquis, C.E. Bosworth, E. van Donzel, and W.P. Heinrichs. Leiden: E.J. Brill, 2012. http://dx.doi.org/10.1163/1573-3912_islam_COM_0375 <20 Aug. 2019>.

Ashraf, S.E. *A Critical Exposition of Iqbal's Philosophy*. Patna, Bihar, India: Associated Book Agency, 1978.

Azad, Hasan. "Reconstructing the Muslim Self: Muhammad Iqbal, Khudi, and the Modern Self." *Islamophobia Studies Journal* 2, no. 2 (2014): 14–28.

Baljon, J.M.S. *The Reforms and Religious Ideas of Sir Sayyid Ahmad Khan*. 2nd ed. Lahore: Orientalia, 1958.

Bausani, Alessandro. "Iqbal: His Philosophy of Religion, and the West." In *Crescent and Green: A Miscellany of Writings on Pakistan*, 131–41. London: Cassell & Co., 1955.

Bernstein, Richard. *Beyond Objectivism and Relativism*. Philadelphia: University of Pennsylvania Press, 1983.

Blitz, David. *Emergent Evolution: Qualitative Novelty and the Levels of Reality*. Dordrecht: Kluwer Academic Publishers, 1992.

Böwering, Gerhard. "The Light Verse: Qur'ānic Text and Ṣūfī Interpretation." *Oriens* 36 (2001): 113–44.

Burney, S.M.H., ed. *Kulliyat Makateeb-e-Iqbal*. 4 vols. Delhi: Urdu Academy, 1989–98.

Byrne, Peter. *Natural Religion and the Nature of Religion: The Legacy of Deism*. London: Routledge, 2013.

Cattelan, Valentino. "Alice's Adventures, Abductive Reasoning and the Logic of Islamic Law." *International Journal for the Semiotics of Law – Revue internationale de sémiotique juridique* 29, no. 2 (2016): 359–88.

Chittick, William C. "The Perfect Man as the Prototype of the Self in the Sufism of Jāmī." *Studia Islamica*, no. 49 (1979): 135–57.

Collingwood, Robin George. *An Autobiography*. London: Oxford University Press, 1939.

Corning, Peter A. "The Re-emergence of Emergence, and the Causal Role of Synergy in Emergent Evolution." *Synthese* 185, no. 2 (2012): 295–317.

Cug̲h̲tā'ī, Muḥammad 'Abdullāh. "'Allāmah Iqbāl Kā Janūbī Hind Kā Safar." In *Muta'alliqāt-i K̲h̲uṭbāt-i Iqbāl*, ed. Sayyid 'Abdullāh, 17–45. Lahore: Iqbal Academy Pakistan, 1977.

Dar, Bashir Ahmad, ed. *Letters of Iqbal*. 3rd ed. Lahore: Iqbal Academy Pakistan, 2015.
– *Religious Thought of Sayyid Ahmad Khan*. Lahore: Institute of Islamic Culture, 1957.
– "Sayyid Ahmad and Modernism." In *Herald of Nineteenth Century Muslim Thought: Sir Sayyid Ahmad Khan*, ed. M. Ikram Chaghatai, 125–30. Lahore: Sang-e-Meel Publications, 2005.
"Death of a Great Indian Muslim Poet." *Times of India*, 22 April 1938.
Deely, John. *Basics of Semiotics*. Bloomington: Indiana University Press, 1990.
– "From Semiosis to Semioethics: The Full Vista of the Action of Signs." *Σημειωτκή – Sign Systems Studies* 36, no. 2 (2008): 437–92.
– *The Impact on Philosophy of Semiotics: The Quasi-error of the External World with a Dialogue between a "Semiotist" and a "Realist"*. South Bend, IN: St Augustine's Press, 2003.
– *Medieval Philosophy Redefined: The Development of Cenoscopic Science, AD 354 to 1644*. Scranton, PA: University of Scranton Press, 2010.
– *New Beginnings: Early Modern Philosophy and Postmodern Thought*. Toronto: University of Toronto Press, 1994.
– "Semiotics 'Today': The Twentieth-Century Founding and Twenty-First-Century Prospects." In *International Handbook of Semiotics*, ed. Peter Pericles Trifonas, 29–113. Dordrecht: Springer, 2015.
Devji, Faisal. "Illiberal Islam." In *Enchantments of Modernity: Empire, Nation, Globalization*, ed. Saurabh Dube, 234–63. New Delhi: Routledge, 2009.
Dewey, John. *Logic: The Theory of Inquiry*. New York: Henry Holt and Company, 1938.
– *The Quest for Certainty: A Study of the Relation of Knowledge and Action*. New York: Minton, Balch, and Company, 1929.
– *Reconstruction in Philosophy*. New York: Henry Holt and Company, 1920.
Diagne, Souleymane Bachir. "Achieving Humanity: Convergence between Henri Bergson and Muhammad Iqbal." In *Muhammad Iqbal: Essays on the Reconstruction of Modern Muslim Thought*, ed. H.C. Hillier and Basit Koshul, 33–55. Edinburgh: Edinburgh University Press, 2015.
– *Islam and Open Society: Fidelity and Movement in the Philosophy of Muhammad Iqbal*. Trans. Melissa McMahon. Dakar: Codesria, 2010.
Enver, Ishrat Hasan. *The Metaphysics of Iqbal*. Lahore: Sh. Muhammad Ashraf, 1944.
Ernst, Waltraud. "Colonial Psychiatry, Magic and Religion. The Case of Mesmerism in British India." *History of Psychiatry* 15, no. 1 (2004): 57–71.
Esdaile, James. *Mesmerism in India and Its Practical Application in Surgery and Medicine*. London: Brown, Green, and Longmans, 1846.
Faizi, Nauman. "Why Saying 'Only Some Muslims Are Violent' Is No Better than Saying 'All Muslims Are Violent.'" In *Scripture and Violence*, ed. Julia Snyder and Daniel H. Weiss, 76–87. New York: Routledge, 2020.

Faruqi, Shamsur Rahman. "How to Read Iqbal?" In *How to Read Iqbal? Essays on Iqbal, Urdu Poetry, and Literary Theory*, ed. Muhammad Suheyl Umar, 3–48. Lahore: Iqbal Academy Pakistan, 2007.

– "Is Iqbal, the Poet, Relevant to Us Today?" In *How to Read Iqbal? Essays on Iqbal, Urdu Poetry, and Literary Theory*, ed. Muhammad Suheyl Umar, 49–58. Lahore: Iqbal Academy Pakistan, 2007.

Făzli, Abdul Hafeez. "Iqbal's View of Omniscience and Human Freedom." *Muslim World* 95, no. 1 (2005): 125–45.

Forster, E.M. "The Poetry of Iqbal." *Athenaeum*, 10 Dec. 1920.

Graham, George Farquhar Irving. *The Life and Work of Sir Syed Ahmed Khan*. Calcutta: Thacker, Spink & Co., 1909.

Griffel, Frank. "Muslim Philosophers' Rationalist Explanation of Muḥammad's Prophecy." In *The Cambridge Companion to Muḥammad*, ed. Jonathan E. Brockopp, 158–79. Cambridge: Cambridge University Press, 2010.

Haack, Susan. "Descartes, Peirce and the Cognitive Community." *Monist* 65, no. 2 (1982): 156–81.

Ḥālī, Alṭāf Ḥusain. *Ḥayāt-i Jāvīd*. 2 vols. Mīrpūr: Arsalān Buks, 2000.

Haq, Syed Nomanul. "Iqbal and Classical Muslim Thinkers." *Iqbal Review* 50 (2009). http://www.allamaiqbal.com/publications/journals/review/aproct09/5.htm <1 Dec. 2020>.

Hartshorne, Charles, and William L. Reese, eds. *Philosophers Speak of God*. Chicago: University of Chicago Press, 1953.

Hasan, Mushirul. *A Moral Reckoning: Muslim Intellectuals in Nineteenth-Century Delhi*. New Delhi: Oxford University Press, 2005.

Hāshimī, Rafī'uddīn. *Taṣānīf-i Iqbāl Kā Taḥqīqī o Tauẓīḥī Muṭāla'ah*. Lahore: Iqbal Academy Pakistan, 1982.

Hassan, Riffat. "Introduction." In *Muhammad Iqbal: Essays on the Reconstruction of Modern Muslim Thought*, ed. H.C. Hillier and Basit Bilal Koshul, 1–11. Edinburgh: Edinburgh University Press, 2015.

– *An Iqbal Primer: An Introduction to Iqbal's Philosophy*. Lahore: Aziz Publishers, 1979.

– "Iqbal's 'Khudi' – Its Meaning and Strengthening Factors." *Iqbal: A Journal of the Bazm-i Iqbal* 23, no. 3 (1976): 1–26.

– "The Main Philosophical Idea in the Writings of Muhammad Iqbal (1877–1938)." Durham, England: Durham University, 1968.

Hillier, H.C. "Iqbal, Bergson and the Reconstruction of the Divine Nexus in Political Thought." In *Muhammad Iqbal: Essays on the Reconstruction of Modern Muslim Thought*, ed. H.C. Hillier and Basit Koshul, 167–200. Edinburgh: Edinburgh University Press, 2015.

– "Theo-political Crisis and Reform: Moses Mendelssohn and Muhammad Iqbal on Law and Society." Toronto: University of Toronto, 2011.

Hillier, H.C., and Basit Bilal Koshul, eds. *Muhammad Iqbal: Essays on the Reconstruction of Modern Muslim Thought*. Edinburgh: Edinburgh University Press, 2015.

Houben, J.J. "The Individual in Democracy and Iqbal's Conception of Khudi." In *Crescent and Green: A Miscellany of Writings on Pakistan*, 142–61. London: Cassell & Co., 1955.

Ḥusain, Riyāẓ. *'Allāmah Muḥammad Iqbāl: Rhodz Laikcarz Dene Kī Da'vat*. Lahore: Iqbal Academy Pakistan, 2012.

Hussain, Khurram. *Islam as Critique: Sayyid Ahmad Khan and the Challenge of Modernity*. New York: Bloomsbury Academic, 2019.

Iqbal, Javed. *Zindah Rūd: 'Allāmah Iqbāl Kī Mukammal Savāniḥ Ḥayāt*. Lahore: Sang-e-Meel Publications, 2004.

Iqbal, Muhammad. "The Doctrine of Absolute Unity as Expounded by Abdul Karim al-Jilani." In *Speeches, Writings, and Statements of Iqbal*, ed. Latif Ahmed Sherwani, 5th ed., 77–97. Lahore: Iqbal Academy Pakistan, 2009.

– "Islam as a Moral and Political Ideal." In *Speeches, Writings, and Statements of Iqbal*, ed. Latif Ahmed Sherwani, 5th ed., 97–117. Lahore: Iqbal Academy Pakistan, 2009.

– "Jug̲h̲rāfiyā'ī Ḥudūd Aur Musalmān." In *Maqālāt-i Iqbāl*, ed. Sayyid 'Abdulvāḥid Mu'īnī, 262–79. Lahore: al-Qamar Inṭarprā'iziz, 2011.

– *Kullīyāt-i Iqbāl*. Lahore: 'Ilm o 'Irfān pablisharz, n.d.

– "The Muslim Community – A Sociological Study." In *Speeches, Writings, and Statements of Iqbal*, ed. Latif Ahmed Sherwani, 5th ed., 118–37. Lahore: Iqbal Academy Pakistan, 2009.

– *Mysteries of Selflessness*. Trans. A.J. Arberry. London: J. Murray, 1953.

– "New Year Message Broadcast from the Lahore Station of All-India Radio on 1st January, 1938." In *Speeches, Writings and Statements of Iqbal*, ed. Latif Ahmed Sherwani, 5th ed., 298–300. Lahore: Iqbal Academy Pakistan, 2009.

– *Payām-i Mashriq*. 10th ed. Lahore: Shaik̲h̲ G̲h̲ulām 'Alī aind Sanz, 1963.

– "Political Thought in Islam." In *Speeches, Writings, and Statements of Iqbal*, ed. Latif Ahmed Sherwani, 5th ed., 138–54. Lahore: Iqbal Academy Pakistan, 2009.

– "Presidential Address Delivered at the Annual Session of the All-India Muslim League, 29th December 1930." In *Speeches, Writings, and Statements of Iqbal*, ed. Latif Ahmed Sherwani, 5th ed., 3–29. Lahore: Iqbal Academy Pakistan, 2009.

– "Presidential Address Delivered at the Annual Session of the All-India Muslim Conference, Lahore, 21st March 1932." In *Speeches, Writings, and Statements of Iqbal*, ed. Latif Ahmed Sherwani, 5th ed., 30–49. Lahore: Iqbal Academy Pakistan, 2009.

– *The Reconstruction of Religious Thought in Islam*. Ed. M. Saeed Sheikh. Stanford, CA: Stanford University Press, 2012.

– *Secrets of the Self: A Philosophical Poem*. Trans. Reynold A. Nicholson. London: Macmillan and Co., Limited, 1920.

– "Self in the Light of Relativity." In *Thoughts and Reflections of Iqbal*, ed. Syed Abdul Vahid, 110–15. Lahore: Sh. Muhammad Ashraf, 1964.

– *Speeches, Writings, and Statements of Iqbal*, ed. Latif Ahmed Sherwani, 5th ed. Lahore: Iqbal Academy Pakistan, 2009.

– "Statement on Islam and Nationalism in Reply to a Statement of Maulana Husain Ahmad, Published in the Ehsan on 9th March, 1938." In *Speeches, Writings, and Statements of Iqbal*, ed. Latif Ahmed Sherwani, 5th ed., 300–13. Lahore: Iqbal Academy Pakistan, 2009.

– *Tashkīl-i Jadīd Ilāhiyāt-i Islāmiyah*. Trans. Nazir Niazi. 5th ed. Lahore: Bazm-i Iqbal, 2000.

Iqbal, Saeeda. "Muhammad Iqbāl's Dynamic Rationalism." In *Islamic Rationalism in the Subcontinent*, 219–330. Lahore: Islamic Book Service, 1984.

Jansen, J.J.G. "Tadjdīd." In *Encyclopaedia of Islam: Second Edition*, ed. P. Bearman, Th. Bianquis, C.E. Bosworth, E. van Donzel, and W.P. Heinrichs. Leiden: E.J. Brill, 2012. http://dx.doi.org/10.1163/1573-3912_islam_SIM_7276 <13 May 2020>.

Kang, Peter. "Mapping Triadic Vistas: A Commentary on the Work of Peter Ochs in Response to Leora Batnitzky." *Journal of Scriptural Reasoning* 8, no. 2 (2009). http://jsr.shanti.virginia.edu/back-issues/vol-8-no-2-august-2009-the-roots-of-scriptural-reasoning/mapping-triadic-vistas/ <14 Aug. 2019>.

Kevelson, Roberta. "Transfer, Transaction, Asymmetry: Junctures between Law and Economics from the Fish-Eye Lens of Semiotics." *Syracuse Law Review* 42, no. 1 (1991): 7–26.

Khan, Abdul Sattar. "A Great Stalwart of the Aligarh Movement: Nawab Mohsin-Ul-Mulk." *Pakistan Annual Research Journal* 49 (2013): 45–58.

Khan, Naveeda. *Muslim Becoming: Aspiration and Skepticism in Pakistan*. Durham, NC: Duke University Press, 2012.

Knysh, Alexander D. *Ibn 'Arabi in the Later Islamic Tradition: The Making of a Polemical Image in Medieval Islam*. Albany: SUNY Press, 1998.

Koshul, Basit Bilal. "Muhammad Iqbal's Reconstruction of the Philosophical Argument for the Existence of God." In *Muhammad Iqbal: A Contemporary*, ed. Muhammad Suheyl Umar and Basit Bilal Koshul, 95–127. Lahore: Iqbal Academy Pakistan, 2010.

Lindbeck, George A. *The Nature of Doctrine: Religion and Theology in a Postliberal Age*. Louisville, KY: Westminster John Knox Press, 2009.

Little, John T. "al-Insān al-Kāmil: The Perfect Man According to Ibn al-'Arabī." *Muslim World* 77, no. 1 (1987): 43–54.

McClure, Christopher Scott. "Reconstructing Islam in a Post-metaphysical Age: Muhammad Iqbal's Interpretation of Immortality." In *Muhammad Iqbal: Essays on the Reconstruction of Modern Muslim Thought*, ed. H.C. Hillier and Basit Koshul, 142–66. Edinburgh: Edinburgh University Press, 2015.

MacDonald, D.B. *The Religious Attitude and Life in Islam*. Chicago: University of Chicago Press, 1909.

MacDonald, D.B., and T. Fahd. "Sīmiyā'." In *Encyclopaedia of Islam: Second Edition*, ed. P. Bearman, Th. Bianquis, C.E. Bosworth, E. van Donzel, and W.P. Heinrichs. Leiden: E.J. Brill, 2012. http://dx.doi.org/10.1163/1573-3912_islam_SIM_7036 <6 Aug. 2019>.

MacDonald, D.B., and W. Madelung. "Malā'ika." In *Encyclopaedia of Islam: Second Edition*, ed. P. Bearman, Th. Bianquis, C.E. Bosworth, E. van Donzel, and W.P. Heinrichs. Leiden: E.J. Brill, 2012. http://dx.doi.org/10.1163/1573-3912_islam_COM_0642 <9 Aug. 2019>.

MacDonald, D.B., H. Massé, P.N. Boratav, K.A. Nizami, and P. Voorhœve. "Dj̲inn." In *Encyclopaedia of Islam: Second Edition*, ed. P. Bearman, Th. Bianquis, C.E. Bosworth, E. van Donzel, and W.P. Heinrichs. E.J. Brill, 2012. http://dx.doi.org/10.1163/1573-3912_islam_COM_0191 <5 Aug. 2019>.

McDonough, Sheila. "Iqbal: His Metaphysical Ideas." In *Hundred Years of Iqbal Studies*, ed. Waheed Ishrat, 403–13. Islamabad: Pakistan Academy of Letters, 2003.

Mackenzie, John S. *An Introduction to Social Philosophy*. 2nd ed. Glasgow: James Maclehose & Sons, 1895.

Majeed, Javed. "Introduction to Muhammad Iqbal's *The Reconstruction of Religious Thought in Islam*." In Muhammad Iqbal, *The Reconstruction of Religious Thought in Islam*, ed. M. Saeed Sheikh, xi–xxx. Stanford, Calif.: Stanford University Press, 2012.

– *Muhammad Iqbal: Islam, Aesthetics, and Postcolonialism*. New Delhi: Routledge, 2009.

– "Putting God in His Place: Bradley, McTaggart, and Muhammad Iqbal." *Journal of Islamic Studies* 4, no. 2 (1993): 208–36.

Malik, Hafeez. "Iqbal's Conception of Ego." *Muslim World* 60, no. 2 (1970): 160–9.

Margoliouth, D.S. *Mohammed and the Rise of Islam*. New York and London: G.P. Putnam's Sons, 1905.

– Review of *The Reconstruction of Religious Thought in Islam*, by Mohammad Iqbal. *Journal of the Royal Asiatic Society of Great Britain and Ireland*, no. 2 (1935): 406–7.

May, Lini S. *Iqbal: His Life and Times*. Lahore: Sh. Muhammad Ashraf, 1974.

Merad, A., Hamid Algar, N. Berkes, and Aziz Ahmad. "Iṣlāḥ." In *Encyclopaedia of Islam: Second Edition*, ed. P. Bearman, Th. Bianquis, C.E. Bosworth, E. van Donzel, and W.P. Heinrichs. Leiden: E.J. Brill, 2012. http://dx.doi.org/10.1163/1573-3912_islam_COM_0386 <12 Sept. 2020>.

Metcalf, Barbara Daly. *Islamic Revival in British India: Deoband, 1860–1900*. Princeton, NJ: Princeton University Press, 1982.

Michot, Yahya. "Revelation." In *The Cambridge Companion to Classical Islamic Theology*, ed. Tim Winter, 180–96. Cambridge: Cambridge University Press, 2008.

Mir, Mustansir. *Iqbal*. Lahore: Iqbal Academy Pakistan, 2006.

Moosa, Ebrahim. "The Human Person in Iqbal's Thought." In *Muhammad Iqbal: Essays on the Reconstruction of Modern Muslim Thought*, ed. H.C. Hillier and Basit Koshul, 12–32. Edinburgh: Edinburgh University Press, 2015.

Morris, Charles W. "Foundations of the Theory of Signs." *International Encyclopedia of Unified Science* 1, no. 2 (1938): 1–59.

Nasr, Seyyed Hossein, ed. *The Study Quran: A New Translation and Commentary*. New York: HarperCollins Publishers, 2015.

Nguyen, Martin. *Modern Muslim Theology: Engaging God and the World with Faith and Imagination*. Lanham, MD: Rowman & Littlefield, 2019.

Niazi, Nazir. "Muqaddamah." In *Tashkīl-i Jadīd Ilāhiyāt-i Islāmiyah*, 5th ed., 7–34. Lahore: Bazm-i Iqbāl, 2000.

Nicholson, R.A. *A Literary History of the Arabs*. New York: Charles Scribner's Sons, 1907.

Noorani, Yaseen. "Islamic Modernity and the Desiring Self: Muhammad Iqbal and the Poetics of Narcissism." *Iran* 38 (2000): 123–35.

– "Muhammad Iqbal and the Immanence of God in Islamic Modernism." *Religion Compass* 8, no. 2 (2014): 60–9.

Nöth, Winfried. *Handbook of Semiotics*. Bloomington: Indiana University Press, 1990.

Ochs, Peter. *Another Reformation: Postliberal Christianity and the Jews*. Grand Rapids, MI: Baker Academic, 2011.

– "Iqbal, Peirce and Modernity." In *Muhammad Iqbal: A Contemporary*, ed. Muhammad Suheyl Umar and Basit Bilal Koshul, 79–92. Lahore: Iqbal Academy Pakistan, 2010.

– *Peirce, Pragmatism, and the Logic of Scripture*. Cambridge: Cambridge University Press, 1998.

– "Reparative Reasoning: From Peirce's Pragmatism to Augustine's Scriptural Hermeneutics." *Modern Theology* 25, no. 2 (2009): 187–215.

– "Re-socializing Scholars of Religious, Theological, and Theo-philosophical Inquiry." *Modern Theology* 29, no. 4 (2013): 201–19.

Ochs, Peter, Nauman Faizi, Jonathan Teubner, and Zain Moulvi. "Value Predicate Analysis: A Language-Based Tool for Diagnosing Behavioral Tendencies of Religious or Value-Based Groups in Regions of Conflict." *Journal for the Scientific Study of Religion* 58, no. 1 (2019): 93–113.

Orsi, Robert A. "The Problem of the Holy." In *The Cambridge Companion to Religious Studies*, ed. Robert A. Orsi, 84–105. New York: Cambridge University Press, 2012.

Peirce, Charles Sanders. *Collected Papers of Charles Sanders Peirce*. Ed. Charles Hartshorne and Paul Weiss. 6 vols. Cambridge, MA: Harvard University Press, 1932–5.

Petrilli, Susan, and Augusto Ponzio. *Semiotics Unbounded: Interpretive Routes through the Open Network of Signs*. Toronto: University of Toronto Press, 2005.

Pickering, Andrew. *The Mangle of Practice: Time, Agency, and Science*. London: University of Chicago Press, 1995.

Pickthall, Marmaduke. "Sir Muhammad Iqbal's Lectures." *Islamic Culture: The Hyderabad Quarterly Review* 5, no. 4 (1931): 677–83.

– *The Cultural Side of Islam*. 2nd ed. Madras: Hilal Press, 1937.

Pink, Johanna. "Striving for a New Exegesis of the Qur'ān." In *The Oxford Handbook of Islamic Theology*, ed. Sabine Schmidtke, 765–92. Oxford: Oxford University Press, 2016.

Rafiuddin, Mohammad. "Iqbal's Idea of the Self." *Iqbal Review* 4, no. 3 (1963). http://allamaiqbal.com/publications/journals/review/oct63/1.htm <13 March 2020>.

Rahbar, Muḥammad Daud. "Sir Sayyid Aḥmad Khān's Principles of Exegesis: Translated from His Taḥrīr Fī 'Uṣūl al-Tafsīr." *Muslim World* 46, no. 2 (1956): 104–12.

Rahman, Fazlur. "Modern Muslim Thought." *Muslim World* 45, no. 1 (1955): 16–25.

Raschid, Salman. *Iqbal's Concept of God*. Karachi: Oxford University Press, 2010.

Reddy, Michael J. "The Conduit Metaphor: A Case of Frame Conflict in Our Language about Language." In *Metaphor and Thought*, ed. Andrew Ortony, 2nd ed., 164–201. Cambridge: Cambridge University Press, 1993.

Reetz, Dietrich. "Enlightenment and Islam: Sayyid Ahmad Khan's Plea to Indian Muslims for Reason." *Indian Historical Review* 14, no. 1–2 (1988): 206–18.

Rizvi, Sajjad. "Between Hegel and Rumi: Iqbal's Contrapuntal Encounters with the Islamic Philosophical Traditions." In *Muhammad Iqbal: Essays on the Reconstruction of Modern Muslim Thought*, ed. H.C. Hillier and Basit Koshul, 112–41. Edinburgh: Edinburgh University Press, 2015.

Rorty, Richard. *Philosophy and the Mirror of Nature*. Princeton, NJ: Princeton University Press, 1980.

Scarcia Amoretti, B. "'Ilm al-Ridjāl." In *Encyclopaedia of Islam: Second Edition*, ed. P. Bearman, Th. Bianquis, C.E. Bosworth, E. van Donzel, and W.P. Heinrichs. Leiden: E.J. Brill, 2012. http://dx.doi.org/10.1163/1573-3912_islam_SIM_3540 <15 Oct. 2019>.

Schimmel, Annemarie. *Gabriel's Wing*. Reprint. Lahore: Iqbal Academy Pakistan, 2003.

– "Man of Light or Superman? A Problem of Islamic Mystical Anthropology." *Diogenes* 37, no. 146 (1989): 124–40.

Sebeok, Thomas A. *A Sign Is Just a Sign*. Bloomington: Indiana University Press, 1991.

– *Signs: An Introduction to Semiotics*. Toronto: University of Toronto Press, 1994.

Seuren, Pieter. *Western Linguistics: An Historical Introduction*. Oxford: Blackwell Publishing, 1998.

Sevea, Iqbal Singh. *The Political Philosophy of Muhammad Iqbal: Islam and Nationalism in Late Colonial India*. Cambridge: Cambridge University Press, 2012.

Shafique, Khurram Ali. *Iqbal: An Illustrated Biography*. Lahore: Iqbal Academy Pakistan, 2006.

– *Iqbāl: Darmiyānī Daur*. Lahore: Iqbal Academy Pakistan, 2012.

– *Iqbāl: Daur-i 'Urūj*. Lahore: Iqbal Academy Pakistan, 2017.

Shah, Farhan A. "Towards a Process-Humanistic Interpretation of Islam: An Examination of Muhammad Iqbal's God Concept." Oslo: University of Oslo, 2016.

Shah, Muhammad Maroof. *Muslim Modernism and the Problem of Modern Science*. Delhi: Indian Publishers' Distributors, 2007.

Sharif, M.M. *About Iqbal and His Thought*. Lahore: Institute of Islamic Culture, 1964.

– "Editorial." *Iqbal: A Journal of the Bazm-i Iqbal* 1, no. 1 (1952): i–ii.

Sheikh, M. Saeed. "Iqbal as a Modern Interpreter of Islam." *Iqbal: A Journal of the Bazm-i Iqbal* 15, no. 3 (1967): 68–78.

Sherwani, Latif Ahmed, ed. *Speeches, Writings, and Statements of Iqbal*, 5th ed. Lahore: Iqbal Academy Pakistan, 2009.

Ṣiddīqī, Laiṣ. "Ah! Iqbāl." *'Alīgaṛh Maigzīn* 16, no. 2 (1938): preliminary pages.

"Sir Muhammad Iqbal." *Times of India*, April 1938.

Sir Syed. See Aḥmad Ḵẖān, Sayyid (Sir Syed).

Smith, Wilfred Cantwell. *Modern Islām in India: A Social Analysis*. Lahore: Minerva Book Shop, 1943.

– *What Is Scripture?* Minneapolis, Minn.: Fortress Press, 2005.

Stjernfelt, Frederik. *Natural Propositions: The Actuality of Peirce's Doctrine of Dicisigns*. Boston: Docent Press, 2014.

Tareen, SherAli. "Narratives of Emancipation in Modern Islam: Temporality, Hermeneutics, and Sovereignty." *Islamic Studies* 52, no. 1 (2013): 5–28.

Taylor, Charles. "Preface." In *Islam and Open Society*, xi–xii. Dakar: Codesria, 2010.

Tayob, Abdulkader. *Religion in Modern Islamic Discourse*. New York: Columbia University Press, 2009.

Tritton, A.S. Review of *The Reconstruction of Religious Thought in Islam*, by Mohammad Iqbal. *Bulletin of the School of Oriental Studies, University of London* 7, no. 3 (1934): 693–5.

Troll, Christian W. *Sayyid Ahmad Khan: A Reinterpretation of Muslim Theology*. New Delhi: Vikas Publishing House, 1978.

– "Sir Sayyid Ahmad Khan, 1817–98, and His Theological Critics: The Accusations of 'Ali Bakhsh Khan and Sir Sayyid's Rejoinder." In *Herald of Nineteenth Century Muslim Thought: Sir Sayyid Ahmad Khan*, ed. M. Ikram Chaghatai, 325–56. Lahore: Sang-e-Meel Publications, 2005.

Umar, Muhammad Suheyl. *Dar-i Ā'īnah Bāz Hai*. Lahore: Iqbal Academy Pakistan, 2009.

– *K̲h̲uṭbāt-i Iqbāl: Na'e Tanāẓur Meṉ* 3rd ed. Lahore: Iqbal Academy Pakistan, 2008.

Van Ess, Josef. "Verbal Inspiration? Language and Revelation in Classical Islamic Theology." In *The Qur'an as Text*, ed. Stefan Wild, 177–94. Leiden: Brill, 1996.

Weiss, Daniel H. *Paradox and the Prophets: Hermann Cohen and the Indirect Communication of Religion*. New York: Oxford University Press, 2012.

Wheeler, Richard S. "Individual and Action in the Thought of Iqbal." *Muslim World* 52, no. 3 (1962): 197–206.

Whittemore, Robert. "Iqbal's Panentheism." *Review of Metaphysics* 9, no. 4 (1956): 681–99.

Wielandt, Rotraud. "Exegesis of the Qur'ān: Early Modern and Contemporary." In *Encyclopaedia of the Qur'ān*, ed. Jane Dammen McAuliffe, vol. 2, 124–42. Leiden: Brill, 2001.

Yelle, Robert A. "Semiotics." In *The Oxford Handbook of the Study of Religion*, ed. Michael Stausberg and Steven Engler, 208–19. Oxford: Oxford University Press, 2016.

Zubairī, Amīn. *Ḥayāt-i Muḥsin*. 'Alīgaṛh: Muslim Yūnīvarsiṭī Prais, 1934.

Index

Adams, Nicholas, 95–7
Ahmad, Aziz, 90
Ahmed, Shahab, 69, 100
Ali, Syed Mehdi, 23–6
al-Insān al-Kāmil, 89

cenoscopy, 98

Deely, John, 52
Dewey, John, 109, 126n52
Diagne, Souleymane Bachir, 108

experience, 47; as three-part relation, 47–52

Forster, E.M., 89

God: biology and, 78–81; Iqbal's proof of, 82; physics and, 76–8; psychology and, 81–2

hermeneutics of war, 40–1, 65, 86
human selfhood (*khudi*): freedom of, 98–100; genealogies of, 89–91; Iqbal's criticism of approaches to, 93–8; Iqbal's style of predicating features to, 101; political aspects of, 92–3; theological aspects of, 91–2

inductive intellect, 109
intellectual test of religious experience, 72–5; cognitive-dissonance model, 74; epistemological model, 72; ontological model, 73
Islam: Iqbal's approach to, 63–5, 104–12

Jesus, 37–8
jinn, 36–7, 133n73

Khan, Naveeda, 92, 100
khudi. *See* selfhood
knowledge, 46; as three-part relation, 47–52

Majeed, Javed, 83, 108
McDonough, Sheila, 91–2
mesmerism, 39
miracles, 31–3, 36–8
Moosa, Ebrahim, 91
Moses, 38–9
mystical experience, 57–61

Noorani, Yaseen, 84

Ochs, Peter, 40–1

Pickthall, Marmaduke, 7
pragmatism, 12–16

reality, 47; as three-part relation, 47–52
religion: Iqbal's contextual approach to, 52–5, 57–60, 66; Iqbal's representationalist approach to, 61–7; as primitive objectivity, 54–5; as primitive subjectivity, 55–6
religious experience. *See* mystical experience
repair, 15–16, 20, 121
representationalism, 9–12, 22–3, 27–9
revelation, 104–12
reviews of *The Reconstruction of Religious Thought in Islam*, 4, 6–8

Schimmel, Annemarie, 90–1
science: Iqbal's approach to, 58–9, 76–87; Sir Syed's approach to, 28, 34–5, 41
scriptural hermeneutics: Iqbal's, 19–20, 112–17; Sir Syed Ahmed Khan's, 32–6
selfhood (*khudi*), 18–19, 68–70, 86
semiotics, 48–52
Sevea, Iqbal Singh, 92, 96
Sir Syed: naturalism, 29–32; principles of exegesis, 29–30; on religion and science, 32–41
Smith, Wilfred Cantwell, 50–1, 95–6

Tayob, Abdulkader, 107–8

Wensinck, A.J., 8
Whittemore, Robert, 84